First World War
and Army of Occupation
War Diary
France, Belgium and Germany

23 DIVISION
70 Infantry Brigade
York and Lancaster Regiment
9th (Service) Battalion
27 August 1915 - 31 October 1917

WO95/2188/2

The Naval & Military Press Ltd
www.nmarchive.com
Published in association with The National Archives

Published by

The Naval & Military Press Ltd

Unit 10 Ridgewood Industrial Park,

Uckfield, East Sussex,

TN22 5QE England

Tel: +44 (0) 1825 749494

www.naval-military-press.com

www.nmarchive.com

This diary has been reprinted in facsimile from the original. Any imperfections are inevitably reproduced and the quality may fall short of modern type and cartographic standards.

© **Crown Copyright**
Images reproduced by permission of The National Archives, London, England, 2015.

Contents

Document type	Place/Title	Date From	Date To
Heading	WO95/2188/2		
Heading	23rd Division 70th Infy Bde 9th Bn York & Lancs Regt 1915 Aug-1917 Oct. To Italy.		
War Diary	Bordon.	27/08/1915	27/08/1915
War Diary	Boulogne	28/08/1915	28/08/1915
War Diary	Nordausques.	29/08/1915	05/09/1915
War Diary	Nordausques & Campagne	06/09/1915	07/09/1915
War Diary	Noote Boom.	08/09/1915	09/09/1915
War Diary	Armentieres.	09/09/1915	11/09/1915
War Diary	Steenwerck.	12/09/1915	13/09/1915
War Diary	L'Armee	14/09/1915	30/09/1915
Miscellaneous	Details of Casualties during September.	20/11/1915	20/11/1915
Heading	Attached 8th Division 70th Infy Bde 23 Div 9th Bn Yorks & Lancs. Oct 1915-Jun 1916		
Heading	8th, Division. 70th, Brigade. 9th, York & Lancs. Oct to Dec. 1915		
Heading	8th Div 9th York & Lancs. Vol : I Oct-Dec 121/7931		
War Diary	L'Armee.	01/10/1915	11/10/1915
War Diary	Estaires	11/10/1915	31/10/1915
Miscellaneous	Details of Casualties during October.		
Miscellaneous	Trip Wire Spring Wire	07/10/1915	07/10/1915
War Diary		01/11/1915	10/11/1915
War Diary	Granny.	10/11/1915	17/11/1915
War Diary	Fleurbaix.	18/11/1915	18/11/1915
War Diary	Granny.	22/11/1915	23/11/1915
War Diary	Steenbecque.	23/11/1915	30/11/1915
Miscellaneous	Details of Casualties during November		
War Diary	Steenbecque.	01/12/1915	31/12/1915
Heading	8th, Division. 70th, Brigade. 9th, York & Lancs. January, 1916		
Miscellaneous	D.A.G. 3rd Echelon	25/02/1916	25/02/1916
Miscellaneous	To Adjutant General G.H.Q.	02/02/1916	02/02/1916
Heading	War Diary of 9th Bn York & Lancaster Regt. From Jun 1. 1916 to Jan 31st 1916. (Volume II. 1st Month).		
War Diary	Ref Map 360. 1/40,000 Steenbecque.	01/01/1916	11/01/1916
War Diary	Trenches.	12/01/1916	31/01/1916
Heading	8th, Division. 70th, Brigade. 9th, York & Lancs. February, 1916		
Heading	War Diary 9th Bn York & Lancaster Regiment. (Vol.2 2nd Month).		
War Diary	Map Rfce 1/40,000 Sheet 36	01/02/1916	29/02/1916
Heading	8th, Division. 70th, Brigade. 9th, York & Lancs. March, 1916		
Heading	War Diary For Month Of March 1916 9th Bn York & Lancaster Regt. Vol II Month 3		
War Diary	Fleurbaix.	01/03/1916	31/03/1916
War Diary	Albert	01/04/1916	30/04/1916
Miscellaneous	Addenda To April. Awards Vol 6		
Miscellaneous	Summary of Casualties. For April		

Heading	8th, Division. 70th, Brigade. 9th, York & Lancs. May, 1916		
Miscellaneous	To officer Ye Infantry Records York	08/06/1916	08/06/1916
War Diary	Trenches.	01/05/1916	11/05/1916
War Diary	Henencourt	12/05/1916	27/05/1916
War Diary	Albert.	28/05/1916	31/05/1916
Miscellaneous	Awards.		
Miscellaneous	Casualties During The Month.		
Heading	8th, Division. 70th, Brigade. 9th, York & Lancs. June, 1916		
War Diary	Albert District.	01/06/1916	30/06/1916
Heading	70th Inf. Bde. 23rd Div. Battn. with Bde. rejoined from 8th Div. 17.7.16. 9th Battn. The York & Lancaster Regiment. July 1916 Attached: Appendices.		
War Diary		01/07/1916	31/07/1916
Heading	Appendices.		
Operation(al) Order(s)	Operation Order No. 1. By Lt. Col. A.B. Addison Commanding 9th Bn York & Lancaster Regt	16/06/1916	16/06/1916
Miscellaneous	Orders For. Movement. Into Assembly Position. 9 Bn York & Lancaster Regt.		
Miscellaneous	Attack Orders.		
Miscellaneous	Issued.	18/06/1916	18/06/1916
Miscellaneous	& Orders In the attack		
Miscellaneous	9th York & Lancaster Rgt.	20/06/1916	20/06/1916
Heading	70th Brigade 23rd Division. 1/9th Battalion Yorks & Lancs Regiment August 1916		
War Diary		01/08/1916	01/06/1917
War Diary	G.24.b.4.5	02/06/1917	30/06/1917
Operation(al) Order(s)	The 9th Bn York & Lancaster Regiment. Operation Order No 2 By Lieut. Colonel J.N. Bowes Wilson Commanding	03/06/1917	03/06/1917
Miscellaneous	Instructions No. 10 Nominal Rolls	03/06/1917	03/06/1917
Miscellaneous	Instructions No. 2 Signalling Communication	03/06/1917	03/06/1917
Miscellaneous	Instructions No 3:- Contact Aeroplane	05/06/1917	05/06/1917
Miscellaneous	Moppers Up.	05/06/1917	05/06/1917
Miscellaneous	Instruction No 4-Rations.	05/06/1917	05/06/1917
War Diary	Line	01/07/1917	31/07/1917
War Diary		27/07/1917	27/07/1917
War Diary		23/07/1917	23/07/1917
War Diary	Meteren.	01/08/1917	05/08/1917
War Diary	Meteren.	03/08/1917	06/08/1917
War Diary	Arques	06/08/1917	06/08/1917
War Diary	Alquines	07/08/1917	09/08/1917
War Diary	Nortleulinghem	09/08/1917	10/08/1917
War Diary	St Janster Beizen.	11/08/1917	23/08/1917
War Diary	Dominion Camp.	24/08/1917	24/08/1917
War Diary	Chateau Segard.	25/08/1917	27/08/1917
War Diary	Zillebeke Bund	27/08/1917	30/08/1917
War Diary	K30.c.3.0	30/08/1917	31/08/1917
War Diary	Wippenhoek	01/09/1917	03/09/1917
War Diary	Oosthoek.	03/09/1917	30/09/1917
War Diary	Menin. Rd.	01/10/1917	03/10/1917
War Diary	Meteren	04/10/1917	08/10/1917
War Diary	Meteren.	05/10/1917	31/10/1917

100 015/2188/2

23RD DIVISION
70TH INFY BDE

9TH BN YORK & LANCS REGT

~~AUG - SEP 1915~~
~~JLY 1916 - 1918~~

1915 AUG — 1917 OCT

TO ITALY

Army Form C. 2118.

9/65 E
XXIII
9th Bn —
9th Bn York Lt. Inf vol I

WAR DIARY
INTELLIGENCE SUMMARY

Aug - Sep '15

Place	Date 1915	Hour	Summary of Events and Information	Remarks and references to Appendices
BORDON.	AUGUST 27th		Battalion left QUEBEC BARRACKS, BORDON, and entrained at LIPHOOK STATION for FOLKESTONE. Disembarked at BOULOGNE at 11.30 p.m.	
BOULOGNE	" 28th	2 A.M.	Battalion arrived in REST CAMP just outside BOULOGNE.	
"	"	5 P.M.	Battalion entrained at PONT de BRIQUES. Transport & machine gun section which crossed via SOUTHAMPTON & HAVRE was on the train.	
"	"	11.30 P.M.	Battalion detrained at AUDRUICQ & marched to Billets at NORDAUSQUES.	
NORDAUSQUES	" 29th to 31st		Battalion in training at NORDAUSQUES.	

J. Adman Lt. Col.
Comdg 9th Bn York & Lancaster Regt.

WAR DIARY
or
INTELLIGENCE SUMMARY.
(Erase heading not required.)

Army Form C. 2118.

Place	Date	Hour	Summary of Events and Information	Remarks and references to Appendices
NORDAUSQUES	Sept 1st		Brigadier General Sir David Kinloch D.S.O. bade farewell to the Battalion owing to his proceeding home to take up another appointment. He expressed his highest appreciation of the BN. & the way in which all ranks of the BN. had loyally supported him through the long & arduous period of training, also his personal sorrow at not being able to lead the Brigade into action.	
"	1st/2nd/5th		Battalion in training at NORDAUSQUES.	
NORDAUSQUES & CAMPAGNE	" 6th	6.0 a 7.70	Battalion left NORDAUSQUES & proceeded to Billets at CAMPAGNE. Remainder of Division billeted roundabout.	
NOOTE BOON	" 8th		Battalion inspected by General Pulteney, Commanding 3rd Corps, who expressed himself as very pleased with the appearance of the Battalion, & he was they handled their arms — & was more that from what he had heard of the Battalion he was quite sure that when the time came all ranks would acquit themselves well.	
"	" 9th		Battalion left NOOTE BOON & marched to ARMENTIERES. Two Companies went to Billets at L'ARMEE & remaining two Companies amalgamated with the 2nd Leinster Regt went into trenches at FERME DU BIEZ. Battalion Head Quarters in ARMENTIERES.	
ARMENTIERES	10th		[illegible handwritten note]	

Army Form C. 2118.

WAR DIARY
or
INTELLIGENCE SUMMARY.
(Erase heading not required.)

Instructions regarding War Diaries and Intelligence Summaries are contained in F. S. Regs., Part II. and the Staff Manual respectively. Title pages will be prepared in manuscript.

Place	Date	Hour	Summary of Events and Information	Remarks and references to Appendices
ARMENTIERES.	Sept 11th		Brigadier General L. F. Phillips D.S.O. took over command of the Brigade.	
STEENWERCK.	12th		Two Companies in Trenches relieved by two Companies in Billets at L'ARMEE (1 company subjected to considerable amount of shelling, but escaped fortunately without any casualties). Went back to Billets at STEENWERCK. A draft of 74 N.C.Os & men awaiting us from 3rd Bn York Lancaster Regt.	
	13th	6 am	Aeroplane fight above STEENWERCK between German & British aeroplanes. German aeroplane eventually brought down.	
L'ARMEE	14th		Battalion marched to Billets at L'ARMEE taking over from the 2nd Bn Royal Irish Regt. The 8th K.O.Y.L.I & 8th York Lancaster Regt occupied Trenches	
	15th			
	16th		with 11th Bn Sherwood Foresters in Close Support. Our Battalion was	
	17th		acting as Battalion in Brigade Reserve to 70th Brigade.	
	18th		Battalion moved into Trenches taking over from 8th K.O.Y.L.I. at Trenches 63, 64, 65, 66. 11th Sherwood Foresters were on our right.	
	22nd		Battalion relieved by 8th K.O.Y.L.I. & moved back into Brigade Reserve with Headquarters at GRISPOT, & three Companies at RUE FLEURIE & one Company at L'ARMEE. Intense bombardment by	
	23rd		our artillery proceeding.	

Army Form C. 2118.

WAR DIARY
or
INTELLIGENCE SUMMARY.
(Erase heading not required.)

Place	Date	Hour	Summary of Events and Information	Remarks and references to Appendices
	Sept 24th		Bombardment continues. Battalion Headquarters moved forward to LA VESSÉE.	
	25th		Opening of LOOS BATTLE. Artillery bombardment from 4.30 am onwards. Battery by Battalion Headquarters at LA VESSÉE was knocked out about 11 am. Company left at L'ARMÉE brought up to RUE FLUERIE POST. LIEUT. H.B. WALKER, R.A.M.C. attached to this Battalion awarded military cross for gallantry in attending wounded at the Battery under heavy fire. RUE FLUERIE ROAD also heavily shelled & the farms occupied by the Bn as billets were considerably knocked about. Under the circumstances the Bn was very fortunate in having only a few casualties. The message received about noon stating that the Battalion was to be ready to move at a moment's notice as reinforcements had been seen advancing from the direction of LILLE. Ammunition was brought up & each man served out with an additional 100 rounds. Battalion stood to in readiness to move at a moment's notice. CASUALTIES: 3 wounded.	

Army Form C. 2118.

WAR DIARY
or
INTELLIGENCE SUMMARY.
(Erase heading not required.)

Instructions regarding War Diaries and Intelligence Summaries are contained in F. S. Regs., Part II. and the Staff Manual respectively. Title pages will be prepared in manuscript.

Place	Date	Hour	Summary of Events and Information	Remarks and references to Appendices
	Apl 26th	4am	Battalion Headquarters returned to GRISPOT. Very little shelling going on	
	" 27th		Battalion returned to trenches taking over 8th K.O.Y.L.I.	
	" 30.		Battalion went into Brigade advanced Reserve Trenches with one Company in Close Support taking over from the 8th York Lancaster Regt. Headquarters at the ORCHARD. LIEUT. E.C. SILLAR killed by German shell. Lt. Sillar was at the time acting as Brigade Grenadier Officer.	
			CASUALTIES DURING MONTH.	
			Officers: 1 killed. Other Ranks: 1 killed, 11 wounded.	

J.H. Moss Lt. Col.
Comdg 9th Bn York & Lancaster Regt.

Army Form C. 2118.

WAR DIARY
or
INTELLIGENCE SUMMARY.
(Erase heading not required.)

Place	Date	Hour	Summary of Events and Information	Remarks and references to Appendices
			Details of Casualties during September.	
			KILLED.	
			Sept. 28: 17035 Pte. Jas. Gilligan	
			" 30: Lieut. T. E. Millar	
			WOUNDED	
			Sept 10: 19144 Pte. Thos. Warner	
			" 11: 18830 " Fred Kelley	
			" 17: 15446 " Arthur Stelell *	
			" 17: 12263 " John Wainwright	
			" 21: 18990 " Hope J. W. Lisle	
			" 25: 18999 Pte. Jas. Schofield	
			" 25: 18869 " John Benton (sewer)	
			" 25: 15375 " Bert Garrett	
			" 28: 15955 " John Bailey	
			* Died on 20.11.15.	
			[signature]	
			Lt.Col.	
			Comdg 9th Bn. York & Lancaster Regt.	

ATTACHED 8TH DIVISION
70TH INFY BDE

23 DIV.

9TH BN YORKS & LANCS.
OCT 1915-JUN 1916

ATTACHED 8TH DIVISION
70TH INFY BDE

8th, Division.

70th, Brigade.

9th, York & Lancs.

Oct to Dec.
1915.

8th R.W.I

9th York Lancs,
Vol: I 9

Oct- Dec/
1931

Army Form C. 2118.

WAR DIARY
or
INTELLIGENCE SUMMARY.
(Erase heading not required.)

Instructions regarding War Diaries and Intelligence Summaries are contained in F. S. Regs., Part II. and the Staff Manual respectively. Title pages will be prepared in manuscript.

Place	Date	Hour	Summary of Events and Information	Remarks and references to Appendices
L'ARMÉE	October 1st		Battalion in Brigade Reserve Trenches with Headquarters at the Orchard.	
	" 2nd		Battalion went into Reserve Billets at L'ARMÉE.	
	" 4th		Battalion went into Trenches at FERME du BIEZ relieving the 8th K.O.Y.L.I. CASUALTIES: 2 privates wounded.	
	" 7th		Some very good patrolling of Enemy's Lines done by 2nd Lt. C. Buxton. CASUALTIES: 2 killed; 1 wounded.	
	" 8th		Battalion went into Brigade Advanced Reserve Trenches with Headquarters at ORCHARD relieving 8th K.O.Y.L.I.	
	" 10th		Battalion went into Divisional Reserve & proceeded for the night to billets at FORT ROMPU.	
	" 11th		Battalion marched to billets at ESTAIRES relieving a Battalion of the 69th Brigade, 70th Brigade in Divisional Reserve to 20th Division.	
ESTAIRES	11th to 17th		Battalion still in Divisional Reserve; good deal of training carried out.	

WAR DIARY
or
INTELLIGENCE SUMMARY.
(Erase heading not required.)

Army Form C. 2118.

Place	Date	Hour	Summary of Events and Information	Remarks and references to Appendices
	Oct. 18th		Battalion proceeded to billets at GRANNY about 1½ miles S.E. of SAILLY MAILLY coming into Divisional Reserve to the 8th Division. From this day onwards the 70th Brigade came under command of Major-General H. Hudson C.B. C.V.E. commanding 8th Division.	
	" 19th		Battalion amalgamated with 2nd Bn Middlesex Regt. Two Platoons from each Company & Coy. Headquarters of "C" & "D" Coys proceeded to billets of 2nd Middlesex Regt. at CUL DE SAC. In exchange 2nd Middlesex Regt sent to this Battalion two platoons per Coy & two Coy Headquarters. Brigade now formed as follows – Amalgamated Battalions 8th & 9th York & Lancaster Regt, 2nd Middlesex Regt, & 2nd Royal Berkshire Regt. The 11th Sherwood Foresters were temporarily transferred to the 23rd Brigade & 8th K.O.Y.L.I. to the 25th Brigade.	
	" 22nd		Companies that were amalgamated with 2nd Bn Middlesex Regt. returned & Battalion reformed at GRANNY. The 70th Brigade now amalgamated with 25th Brigade. The Brigade comprised as follows:– 8th York & Lancaster Regt, 9th York & Lancaster Regt, 2nd Lincoln Regt, 2nd Rifle Brigade. The 8th K.O.Y.L.I. & 11th Sherwood Foresters transferred to 23rd Brigade.	

Army Form C. 2118.

WAR DIARY
or
INTELLIGENCE SUMMARY.
(Erase heading not required.)

Place	Date	Hour	Summary of Events and Information	Remarks and references to Appendices
	Oct 23rd		Battalion went into Trenches taking over from 2nd West Yorkshire Regt. Battalion French Headquarters at EATON HALL, close to CROIX BLANCHE. The line of Trenches extended from right of salient by CELLAR FARM to right of 8th Middlesex Regt by the CONVENT. On the right of the 8th Middlesex Regt were 8th York Lancaster Regt. Three Companies of the Battalion were in first line Trenches & one Company in close support & occupying CORDONNERIE & DEE POSTS. 8th K.O.Y.L.I. were in Brigade Reserve to us with one forward company in local reserve. CASUALTIES: 1 wounded.	
	" 24th		2nd Lincoln Regt relieved 8th K.O.Y.L.I who were in Brigade Reserve. CASUALTIES: 3 wounded.	
	" 25th		Enemy very quiet. CASUALTIES: 1 wounded.	

Army Form C. 2118.

WAR DIARY
or
INTELLIGENCE SUMMARY.
(Erase heading not required.)

Instructions regarding War Diaries and Intelligence Summaries are contained in F.S. Regs., Part II. and the Staff Manual respectively. Title pages will be prepared in manuscript.

Place	Date	Hour	Summary of Events and Information	Remarks and references to Appendices
	Oct 26th 27th		Two of our Lewis & machine Guns exchanged for two German machine Guns. Scouts of the 2nd Scottish Rifles. The Maxim Gun apparently seemed to draw a good deal of fire during the night. Our Snipers claimed to have shot several German Snipers.	
	"28"		Battalion relieved by 2nd Bn Lincoln Regt. proceeded into Brigade Reserve at RUE du QUESNE; Headquarters at WEATHERCOCK HOUSE with one Company forward in Local reserve to 2nd Bn Lincoln Regt in RUE du BOIS.	
	29th 30th 31st		Battalion still in Brigade Reserve at RUE du QUESNE.	
	"31st"		Battalion proceeded to trenches relieving 2nd Lincoln Regt.	

J. Allan Lt Col
Comdg 9th Bn East Lancaster Regt.

Details of Casualties during October.

KILLED.

Oct 7: 19096 Pte Saml. Pearson
" 7: 19093 C.Q.M.S. Prentice J.H.
" 24: 11579 Christopher Ford

WOUNDED

Oct 4: Pt 15634 Pte. Wm Eckert
" 4: 15633 " Wm. Shub
" 7: 16135 " J. Loodemore
" 23: 15635 " Frank O'Balls.
" 24: 16254 " R Davies
" 24: 10273 " F. Clarke.
" 25: 10547 " W. Watson

Ilwin Lt. Col
Cdg. 9th Bn York & Lancaster Regt.

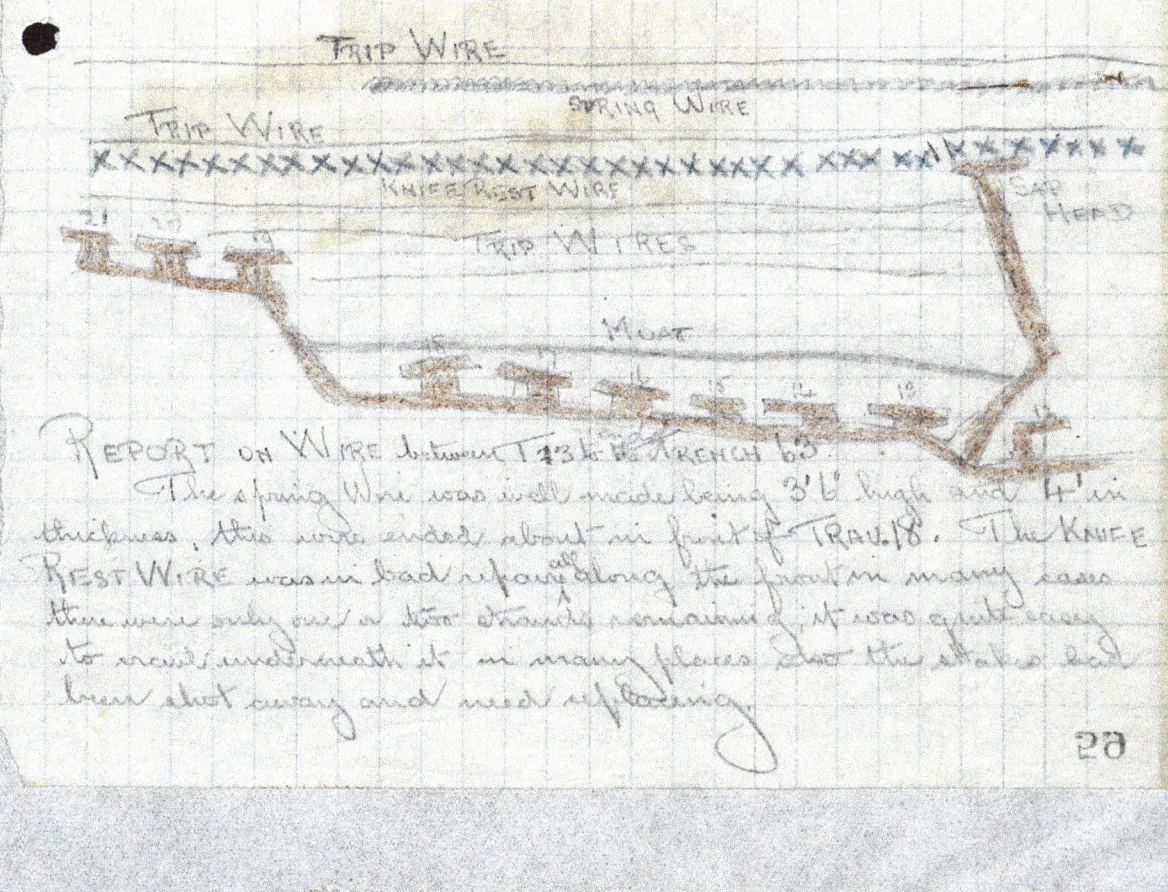

REPORT on WIRE between T.13 & TRENCH 63.
The spring wire was well made being 3'6" high and 4' in thickness, this wire ended about in front of TRAV.18. The Knife Rest Wire was in bad repair all along the front in many cases there were only one or two strands remaining. It was quite easy to crawl underneath it in many places. Also the stakes had been shot away and need replacing.

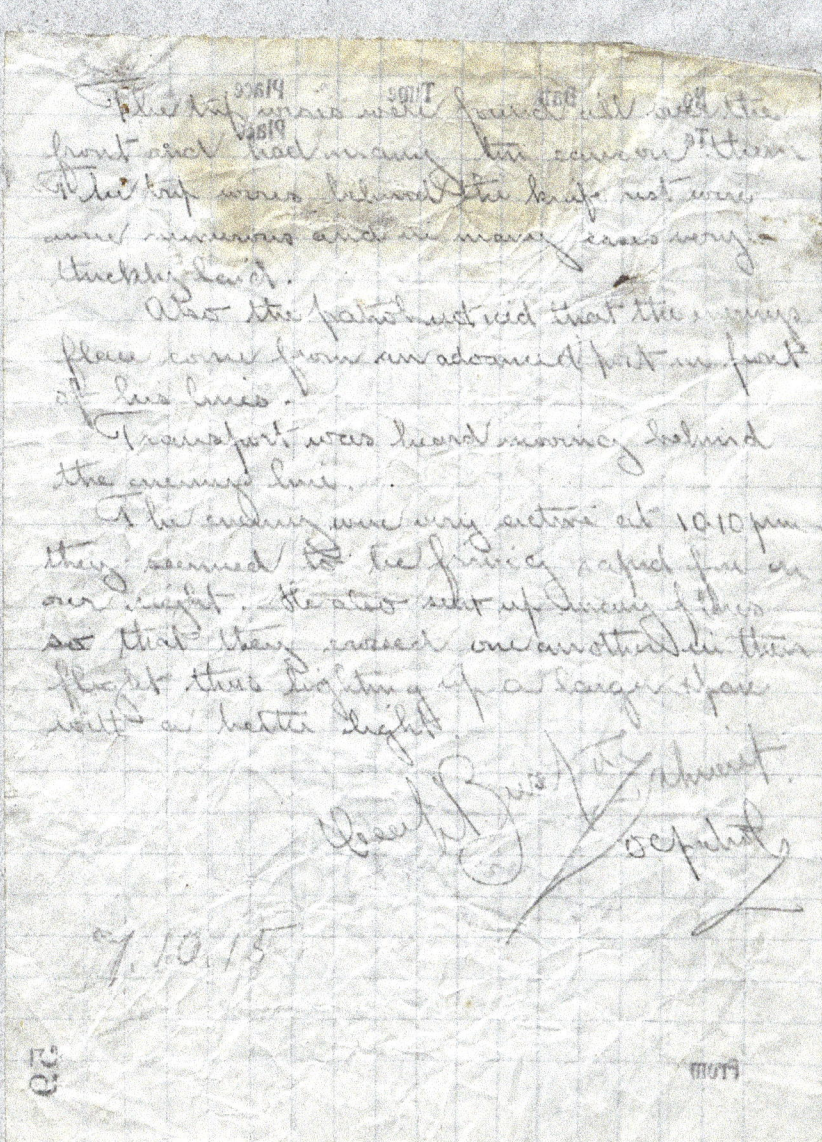

The trip wires were found all along the front and had many tin cans on them. The trip wires behind the knife rest wire were numerous and in many cases very thickly laid.

Was the patrol noticed that the weary flare came from an advanced post in front of his lines.

Transport was heard moving behind the enemy line.

The enemy were very active at 10.10 pm they seemed to be firing rapid fire on our right. He also sent up many flares so that they crossed one another in their flight thus lighting up a larger space with a better light.

Lieut Bristow Edmunds
 Coy Lieut

7.10.15

Army Form C. 2118.

WAR DIARY
or
INTELLIGENCE SUMMARY.
(Erase heading not required.)

Instructions regarding War Diaries and Intelligence Summaries are contained in F.S. Regs., Part II. and the Staff Manual respectively. Title pages will be prepared in manuscript.

Place	Date	Hour	Summary of Events and Information	Remarks and references to Appendices
	Nov. 1st			
	2nd & 3rd		Owing to heavy rains parapet fell in somewhat at MINE AVENUE. CASUALTIES: Killed 1; Wounded 2.	
	4th	7 p.m.	Battalion relieved by 2nd Lincoln Regt. Battalion returns to Brigade Reserve with Billet at WEATHERCOCK HOUSE and neighbourhood.	
	5th		Lt. Col. J. O. Travers, C.M.G. & D.S.O. of 2nd Devon Regt. took over temporary command of the Brigade.	
	7th & 8th		Battalion proceeded to trenches again taking over from 2nd Lincoln Regt. 1/8th Middlesex Regt. T.F. on our left; 2nd Middlesex Regt. in Brigade Reserve. The Battalion was the Right Battalion of the Brigade.	
	8th		General H. Gordon, D.S.O. 2nd Leicestershire Regt. took over command of the Brigade.	
	9th		2nd Lincoln Regt. & 2nd Rifle Brigade rejoined 25th Brigade being replaced by 8th K.O.Y.L.I. & 11th Sherwood Foresters, the 8th K.O.Y.L.I. thereby coming into Brigade Reserve to us in place of the 2nd Lincoln Regt. The 70th Brigade now comprised as when we left ENGLAND. CASUALTIES: Wounded 2.	

Army Form C. 2118.

WAR DIARY
or
INTELLIGENCE SUMMARY.
(Erase heading not required.)

Place	Date	Hour	Summary of Events and Information	Remarks and references to Appendices
GRANNY.	Nov 10th		Brigade goes into Divisional Reserve. This battalion relieved by the 2nd Scottish Rifles. Battalion goes into billets at GRANNY.	
	10th to 17th		Battalion still in Divisional Reserve.	
FLEURBAIX.	18th		The 70th Brigade relieved 25th Brigade in left Brigade area. The Battalion relieved 2nd Lincoln Regt who were in Brigade Reserve & took over then billets in FLEURBAIX. The 8th K.O.Y.L.I. & 11th Sherwood Foresters were in Trenches in front line. 8th Battalion York Lancaster Regt in Brigade Reserve on our right.	
GRANNY.	"22nd		Battalion returned to Brigade Reserve billets at GRANNY on the right. Brigade marched to VIEUX BERQUIN & were billeted there for the night. On way to Corps Reserve.	
	"23rd			
STEENBECQUE.	Nov 24th		Battalion marched into Camp at STEENBECQUE. Battalion marched very well without one man falling out on the two days march. Battalion Camp in a field about ½ mile N.E. of Steenbecque. 18th Middlesex Regt. T.F. in a camp in adjoining field. 8th K.O.Y.L.I.	

WAR DIARY
or
INTELLIGENCE SUMMARY.

Army Form C. 2118.

Place	Date	Hour	Summary of Events and Information	Remarks and references to Appendices
STEENBECQUE.	Nov. 26th to 30th		8th York Lancaster Regt in Billets in STEENBECQUE & roundabout. The 11th Sherwood Foresters in Camp about ½ mile N.W. of STEENBECQUE. Brigade Headquarters in STEENBECQUE. Battalion still in G.86.Q are at STEENBECQUE undergoing constant progressive training — especially in the attack of Trenches.	

JHMan Lt. Col.
Comdg 9th York Lancaster Regt.

Army Form C. 2118.

WAR DIARY
or
INTELLIGENCE SUMMARY.
(Erase heading not required.)

Summary of Events and Information

Details of Casualties during November

KILLED.

Nov. 2: 16919 Pte Y. Turner

WOUNDED.

Nov. 2. 18313 Pte A. Rydall.
" 3. 14516 " A. Banks
" 9. 12414 " Bart O'Brien
" 11. 14763 " J. Langley
" 11. 19062 Cpl. J. Haycock.

Sherwin Lt. Col.
Cdg 9th Bn York. Lancaster Regiment

Army Form C. 2118.

WAR DIARY
or
INTELLIGENCE SUMMARY.
(Erase heading not required.)

Instructions regarding War Diaries and Intelligence Summaries are contained in F. S. Regs. Part II. and the Staff Manual respectively. Title pages will be prepared in manuscript.

Place	Date	Hour	Summary of Events and Information	Remarks and references to Appendices
STEENBECQUE	Dec 1st to 5th		Training of Battalion in Corps Reserve continues, special attention being paid to Bombing and steadying drill and attack of trenches	
	" 6th		2nd Lt R.D Fenton & A.G. Price joined the Battalion this day.	
	" 7th to 10th		Battalion still in training at STEENBECQUE.	
	" 10th		A draft of 21 men joined the Battalion, 18 of these being men who had been in hospital from this Battalion.	
	" 12th		2nd Lt S.A. Bryan joined the Battalion this day.	
	" 13th to 20th		Training in Corps Reserve continues.	
	" 20th		2nd Lt Ellen struck off strength of Battalion having gone to England sick.	
	" 20th		Divisional manoeuvres commenced. The Division marched in the direction of WARDRECQUES. Battalion camped for the night in camp of 2nd Bn. Royal Irish Rifles on the Roman Road close to SERCUS.	
	" 21st		Battalion passed Brigade starting point at WARDRECQUES at 10.40 a.m. & marched with the Division in column of route to CLARQUES. The Brigade	

WAR DIARY
or
INTELLIGENCE SUMMARY.
(Erase heading not required.)

Army Form C. 2118.

Place	Date	Hour	Summary of Events and Information	Remarks and references to Appendices
	Dec 22		Took up a position for attack on hills N.E. of THÉROUANNE. As soon as translating was in position orders were received to proceed to billets for the night. Battalion went into billets at MAMETZ. Battalion moved off at 9.30 a.m. & took up position on hills west of ENGUINEGATTE. A retirement was then practised by the Brigade as far as the BASSE – BOULOGNE & THÉROUANNE ROAD. At 4.30 p.m. Battalion marched via THÉROUANNE & ROQUETOIRE to billets at COHEN. A.S.C. & Artillery were billeted in the village billets were not good.	
	Dec 23rd		Battalion marched via RACQUINGHEM, WARDRECQUES STATION & LA BELYE HOTESSE to camp at STEENBECQUE, arriving at about 2 p.m.	
	Dec 24th 25th 26th		Medical Officer sent 70 Bengalis had less inspections than any other Brigade during its 3 days ad. till the last than the last number of cases in the Brigade. No training carried out during Christmas. Excellent Christmas dinner provided for the men.	
	" 27th to 31st		Training of Battalion continues.	

Signed
Comdg 9th [?] York & Lancaster Regt.

8th, Division.

70th, Brigade.

9th, York & Lancs.

January, 1916.

D.A.G.
3rd Echelon.

Passed to you.
O.C. 9th Bn York &
Lancaster Regt. has
been informed that his
War Diary should be
despatched to your
office & not here

C H Frith Maj
D.A.A.G. for A.G.

g&a
25-2-16

To Adjutant General
           G.H.Q.

Herewith War Diary for
9th Bn York & Lancaster Regt.
for month of January 1916.

                M Lewis
              Capt & adjt
9th Bn York & Lancaster Regt.

Army Form C. 2118

WAR DIARY
or
INTELLIGENCE SUMMARY

(Erase heading not required.)

WAR DIARY

OF

9th Bn. YORK & LANCASTER REGT.

From Jan 1. 1916. To Jan 31st 1916.

(Volume II. 1st part).

Army Form C. 2118.

WAR DIARY
or
INTELLIGENCE SUMMARY.
(Erase heading not required.)

Place	Date	Hour	Summary of Events and Information	Remarks and references to Appendices
REF MAP 36c 1/40,000 STEENBECQUE	1916 JAN 6th		Battalion still in training at STEENBECQUE.	
	" 7th		Arrangements being made for move back to forward area. 2nd Lt. W. Thomas & 2nd Lt. J. Thompson joined the Bn this day.	
	" 8th		Advance Party of 1 Officer & 10 N.C.O.s " arrived from the King's own Yorks't Regt. 51st Bde. to take over Camp.	
	" 9th		Advance Party that arrived yesterday sent to 11th Sherwood Foresters Camp E. of STEENBECQUE. Camp taken over by Officer of 7th K.O.Y.L.I. who was taking over the 8th Middlesex Camp next door.	
	" 10th		Battalion paraded at 8.15 am & marched via LA PARÉ, FORÊT de NIEPPE, NEUF BERQUIN to billets at ESTAIRES arriving about 3 p.m.	
	" 11th		Battalion marched off from ESTAIRES at 1 p.m. & marched with intervals between Companies to CRANNY, after a halt of over an hour the Battalion moved off by Platoons at four minute intervals to take over Trenches N 91. to N 195. from the 6th & 2nd Oxfordshire & Bucks Light Infantry. "D" & "B" Coys went into front line, "A" Coy in RUE PETILLON line Posts & "C" Coy in reserve at RUE de BOIS. The 9th K.O.Y.L.I. were in the trenches on our right & the 8th York Lancasters on the 14th Sherwood trenches in this relieve. The enemy was fairly quiet but rather more during the hour when the Battalion was last in this line. At about 11pm there was some Artillery fire on our left.	

Army Form C. 2118

WAR DIARY
or
INTELLIGENCE SUMMARY
(Erase heading not required.)

Instructions regarding War Diaries and Intelligence Summaries are contained in F. S. Regs., Part II. and the Staff Manual respectively. Title Pages will be prepared in manuscript.

Place	Date	Hour	Summary of Events and Information	Remarks and references to Appendices
TRENCHES.	Jan 12th		Enemy fairly quiet during the day. In the evening a demonstration was made by the Queen's Division on our right with Artillery, rapid machine gun and rifle fire. In retaliation the enemy shelled our 70 yards line and CELLAR FARM AVENUE. CASUALTIES: 1 killed, 1 wounded.	
"	13th		A machine gun first burst of fire at out Salient during the morning. Enemy artillery active on our left between 11am & 12 pm. Our snipers & observers under Sgt. Barley, 'D' Coy now properly organised & distributed along the line, some good work being done.	
"	14th		The enemy artillery again active on our left. Two officers of the 8th Bn York & Lancaster Regt. being hit, one officer dying of his wounds. CASUALTIES: 1 wounded.	
"	15th		Enemy quiet during day. In the evening Battalion relieved by 6th York & Lancaster Regt. The Battalion went into Brigade Reserve billets with Headquarters at JERRY VILLA, H 26 a 4.8. Two Coys in billets at RUE du QUESNE, 1 Coy in CROIX BLANCHE & 1 Coy in billet RUE DU BOIS acting as Reserve Coy to 8th Y & L Regt. CASUALTIES: 1 wounded at about 6 am a German patrol was taken near our wire. He was an under-officer of the 21st Reserve Bavarian Regt. He stated that he had lost his way on Patrol.	

1875 Wt. W593/825 1,000,000 4/15 J.B.C. & A. A.D.S.S./Forms/C. 2118.

WAR DIARY
or
INTELLIGENCE SUMMARY
(Erase heading not required.)

Army Form C. 2118

Place	Date	Hour	Summary of Events and Information	Remarks and references to Appendices
	Jan 16th		An uneventful day. Battalion still in Brigade Reserve Billets.	
	"17th & 18th"		Battalion still in Brigade Reserve. CASUALTIES: 1 wounded.	
	"19th"		In return for bombardment by our artillery orders went on during the morning the enemy dropped a number of shells in the vicinity of RUE DU BOIS. A farm at about N 3 a 2.6. was set on fire by shrapnel at about 3 p.m. & continued to burn for some time. There was apparently a store of S.A.A. in the farm. In the evening the Battalion went into the Front Line Trenches taking over from the 8th York Lancaster Rgt, the 8th K.O.Y.L.I. being on our right again.	
	20th		The enemy unusually quiet all day. Their artillery exceedingly active between 10 am. & 12 noon. About 50 shells dropped in the vicinity of houses at H. 33 & 2.3. many direct hits being obtained. At about 11.45 a.m. house caught fire & was burnt to the ground. This house was being used as the R.W. Medical Aid Post. At about 1 p.m. about 30 shells were dropped in and around EATON HALL twelve direct hits being obtained. There were no casualties but a certain amount	

Army Form C. 2118

WAR DIARY
or
INTELLIGENCE SUMMARY
(Erase heading not required.)

Instructions regarding War Diaries and Intelligence Summaries are contained in F. S. Regs., Part II. and the Staff Manual respectively. Title Pages will be prepared in manuscript.

Place	Date	Hour	Summary of Events and Information	Remarks and references to Appendices
	20th (con.)		of damage was done to the house rendering it impossible for the men any rest. Owing the Barn to be used as a sleeping place for the men any rest. During the evening fires at H.33 d 10.b. was shelled & set alight & continued to burn throughout the night & by next morning it was completely burnt down. CASUALTIES: 4 O.R. wounded.	
	21st		Enemy artillery much quieter to-day. Several shells during the morning were dropped at H.33 d. 6.1. all of them landing in a field. Here 4 O.R. wounded.	
	22nd		It was rather foggy until about 9 o'clock in the morning. Enemy artillery were shelling well behind our lines in the direction of SAILLY all the afternoon.	
	23rd		The Bn was relieved in the Trenches by the 8th Bn Y&L Regt. Bn went into Bde Reserve Billets with Headquarters at JERRY VILLA. About 11.30 p.m. heavy rifle fire & machine gun fire was heard. S.O.S. was sent through from the Sherwood Foresters lines but this was afterwards cancelled.	
	24th & 25th		The Bn still in Bde Reserve. Very little artillery action.	
	26th		The Bde was relieved by the 25th Infantry Brigade & moved back into Divisional Reserve. The 2nd Lincolns relieved this Bn & Hd	

WAR DIARY
or
INTELLIGENCE SUMMARY

(Erase heading not required.)

Army Form C. 2118

Place	Date	Hour	Summary of Events and Information	Remarks and references to Appendices
	26th (con).		Bn moved back after dusk to billets in the vicinity of CUL DE SAC G.8. Bde Headquarters moved to SAILLY CROSS ROADS.	
	27th		Bn still in Divisional Reserve	
	28th		" " " " Training carried out in Arms Drill, musketry, etc.	
	29th		" " " " " " " "	
	30th		" " " " " " " "	
	31st		" " " " " " " "	

Summary of Casualties for the month.

Killed.
4222 Pte Hodges H.

Wounded.
18896 Pte W. Heggitt.
18804 " J. Lloyd.
18839 " J. Butler.
18581 " J. Hanson
10668 " J. Beetham
18912 " Z. Hemsworth.
12382 " W. Wild.
16196 " H. Johnson.

Shannon Lt. Col.
Comdg 9th Bn York & Lancaster Regt.

8th, Division.

70th, Brigade.

9th, York & Lancs.

February, 1916.

Army Form C. 2118.

WAR DIARY
or
INTELLIGENCE SUMMARY.
(Erase heading not required.)

WAR DIARY

9th Bn. York Lancaster Regiment.

(Vol. 2 2nd month).

Army Form C. 2118

WAR DIARY
or
INTELLIGENCE SUMMARY
(Erase heading not required.)

Instructions regarding War Diaries and Intelligence Summaries are contained in F. S. Regs., Part II. and the Staff Manual respectively. Title Pages will be prepared in manuscript.

Place	Date 1916	Hour	Summary of Events and Information	Remarks and references to Appendices
MAP RFCE 40000 Sheet 36	Feb. 1		Battalion still in Divisional Reserve at Cul de Sac Farm.	
	" 2			
	" 3rd		Battalion took over lines of Trenches N 4/1 to N 5/4 from the 2nd Scottish Rifles, 23rd Brigade. 11th Sherwood Foresters took over from 2nd Devonshire Regt. on our left. The 8th York & Lancaster Regt. were in Brigade Reserve to us with Headquarters at FERRETS HOUSE. (M 27 c. 2. 1.) & the 8th K.O.Y.L.I. went into Brigade Reserve to the left Bn with Headquarters at M 21 c. 9.9. Brigade Headquarters in FLEURBAIX. Enemy machine guns traversed our parapet somewhat during the night but this does not look very long. Headquarters of the 4th Tyneside Scottish & half of the Company officers & N.C.O's were attached to this Battalion for instruction.	
	" 4th		A good deal of artillery activity. Between 9 am & 3 pm & shortly after 1 pm three of them were shelled at H. 35 a. 17 were shelled	

Army Form C. 2118

WAR DIARY
or
INTELLIGENCE SUMMARY
(Erase heading not required.)

Instructions regarding War Diaries and Intelligence Summaries are contained in F.S. Regs., Part II. and the Staff Manual respectively. Title Pages will be prepared in manuscript.

Place	Date	Hour	Summary of Events and Information	Remarks and references to Appendices
	Feb 5th		burnt to the ground. LA BOUTILLERIE was heavily shelled at 1 p.m. At 6.15 p.m. enemy shelled CONVENT WALL & Trenches N 5/3 & N 5/4. No damage was done. This artillery activity in the evening was probably in retaliation as our artillery had been shelling enemy wire & parapet between TURK POINT & WATER FORT all the afternoon. Enemy infantry were much more active at Stand-To in the morning & in the evening. RUE DAVID was again shelled during the morning. ELBOW FARM was shelled during the afternoon. Two sections of 4th Tyneside Scottish were attached to each platoon in the front line.	
	6th		Enemy quieter during the day. At 6.15 p.m. enemy dropped several shells on CROIX MARECHAL & also on DUMP at head of TIN BARN TRAMWAY. CASUALTIES: 2 O.R. wounded.	

Army Form C. 2118

WAR DIARY
or
INTELLIGENCE SUMMARY
(Erase heading not required.)

Instructions regarding War Diaries and Intelligence Summaries are contained in F. S. Regs., Part II. and the Staff Manual respectively. Title Pages will be prepared in manuscript.

Place	Date	Hour	Summary of Events and Information	Remarks and references to Appendices
	26.7.4		A quiet day. An enemy working party was seen working behind enemy parapet during the afternoon & was dispersed by artillery fire. In the evening the 8th Bn York & Lancasters Regt relieved us in the Trenches. The Bn went into Bde Reserve in FLEUR BAIX. Attacked portions of the 4th Tyneside Regt. arrived in the Trenches & were attached to the 8th Y&L Regt. CASUALTIES: 1 O.R. killed.	
	8th		The Bn resting in billets.	
	9th		A good deal of shelling in the vicinity of CROIX MARECHAL. Otherwise a quiet day. Headquarters & two Coys of the Tyneside Irish (27th Northumberland Fusiliers) arrived during the afternoon & were attached to this Bn for instruction. CASUALTIES: 1 Officer & 1 O.R. killed.	
	10th		Bn still in Brigade Reserve. Headquarters & half the Coy Officers & N.C.O's & two Companies of the Tyneside Irish went into the	

WAR DIARY
or
INTELLIGENCE SUMMARY

(Erase heading not required.)

Army Form C. 2118

Place	Date	Hour	Summary of Events and Information	Remarks and references to Appendices
	Feb 11th		Trenches to be attacked to the 8th York Lancaster Regt. CASUALTIES: 1 O.R. wounded. The RN relieved the 8th York Regt in the Trenches. Enemy exceedingly quiet all night. The two companies of the Tyneside Irish attached to the 8th RN York Regt in the Trenches remained behind & were attached to us.	
	" 12th		Quiet day on our front but considerable artillery activity on our flanks.	
	" 13th		Some very heavy shelling in the Sherwood Foresters line on our left. Quiet day for us. CASUALTIES: 1 Officer wounded.	
	" 14th		Exceptionally quiet day. Our artillery shelled hostile front line of points N.5/1. The attached Coys of the Tyneside Irish moved out of the Trenches & marched to Rillett at RUE MARLE (Armentières)	

Army Form C. 2118

WAR DIARY
or
INTELLIGENCE SUMMARY
(Erase heading not required.)

Instructions regarding War Diaries and Intelligence Summaries are contained in F. S. Regs., Part II. and the Staff Manual respectively. Title Pages will be prepared in manuscript.

Place	Date	Hour	Summary of Events and Information	Remarks and references to Appendices
	Feb 15th		Battalion relieved by the 8th Bn. Y&L Regt. & returned to Bde. Reserve Billets.	
	" 16th " 17 " 18		Bn in Bde Reserve. No hostile shelling.	
	" 19th		The Bn went into the Trenches again taking over usual line from 8th Y&L Regt. Enemy infantry seemed much more active than usual during the night. At about 10.45 p.m. several aeroplanes were heard passing overhead. One dropped white lights as it passed over enemy's line. CASUALTIES; 1 O.R. wounded.	
	" 20th		Fairly quiet day. Several rounds were fired on a house in RUE DAVID at 2 p.m. At about 2 p.m. 16 of our aeroplanes crossed enemy's lines in direction of LILLE. They were heavily shelled by enemy anti-aircraft guns. CASUALTIES; 1 O.R. wounded	

Army Form C. 2118

WAR DIARY
or
INTELLIGENCE SUMMARY
(Erase heading not required.)

Instructions regarding War Diaries and Intelligence Summaries are contained in F.S. Regs., Part II. and the Staff Manual respectively. Title Pages will be prepared in manuscript.

Place	Date	Hour	Summary of Events and Information	Remarks and references to Appendices
	Feb 21st		Enemy artillery fired a great number of H.E. shells at the CONVENT WALL close to FLAG ALLEY but no damage was done. At evening stand-To enemy harassed our parapet with Machine Guns. There was also a considerable amount of rifle fire.	
	Feb 22nd		Enemy very quiet during the day with the exception of few shells being dropped in vicinity of FLAG ALLEY & MILL ROAD POST. At 10.47 p.m. we commenced a demonstration composed of rapid rifle & machine gun fire, trench mortars, & artillery. The French Mortars directed their fire on TURK POINT. Two direct hits on the parapet were obtained. Three separate bursts of fire were opened the last two burst being accompanied by salvos from the artillery on the enemy front line. The enemy's reply was very weak.	
	23rd		Bn relieved in the Trenches by 8th Y & L Regt. We went back to old billets in FLEURBAIX.	

WAR DIARY
or
INTELLIGENCE SUMMARY

(Erase heading not required.)

Army Form C. 2118

Place	Date	Hour	Summary of Events and Information	Remarks and references to Appendices
	Feb 24		Bn in Brigade Reserve.	
	" 25th		" " " CASUALTIES: 1 O R wounded.	
	" 26th		" " "	
	" 27th		We relieved the 8th Bn Y & L Regt taking over the same line as before. A quiet night. NO MAN'S LAND was reported to be in a very marshy condition owing to the thaw.	
	" 28th		Enemy infantry quiet all day except for a deal of rifle fire at one of our aeroplanes flying rather low in rear of our lines at 10.30 a.m. Enemy artillery shelled FLAG ALLEY and CONVENT WALK at 5 pm. No damage was done.	
	" 29th		Hostile artillery was active all day shelling well back behind our line. There was no shelling of our front line or posts. We fired several ball grenades & hewton Rifle grenades at enemy	

WAR DIARY
or
INTELLIGENCE SUMMARY
(Erase heading not required.)

Army Form C. 2118

Summary of Events and Information

target during the day. Several hits on the parapet being obtained. Bursts of rifle & machine gun fire were opened on CLAPHAM JUNCTION during the night where apparently the enemy has been putting out new wire. CASUALTIES: 1 O.R. wounded.

SUMMARY OF CASUALTIES.

Killed.
- 16150 Hope Kennedy J.
- 19184 Pte G. A. Shaw
- 19220 " W. Littlewood.

Wounded.
- 15295 R.S.M. J. Collinson
- 15032 L/Cpl. D. Jones
- 15497 Pte W. Watson
- 8742 Sgt E. Horley
- 10429 Pte R. Monks
- 19224 Pte H. Barton
- 2nd Lt. D. Radcliff
- 16859 Pte G. W. Rynvater
- 14811 " G. Royston
- 18991 " F. Lewis

J. Allison
Lt Col.
Comdg 9th Bn York Regt.

8th, Division.

70th, Brigade.

9th, York & Lancs.

March, 1916.

Army Form C. 2118

WAR DIARY
or
INTELLIGENCE SUMMARY

(Erase heading not required.)

War Diary

for month of March 1916

9th Bn York & Lancaster Regt.

Vol II Month 3.

Army Form C. 2118

WAR DIARY
or
INTELLIGENCE SUMMARY

(Erase heading not required.)

Instructions regarding War Diaries and Intelligence Summaries are contained in F.S. Regs., Part II. and the Staff Manual respectively. Title Pages will be prepared in manuscript.

Place	Date	Hour	Summary of Events and Information	Remarks and references to Appendices
FLEURBAIX	1st		A quiet day. At evening stand to the enemy machine guns were very active indeed & traversed our parapet up & down from 6.15 pm till about 6.45 pm. CASUALTIES: 1 O.R. wounded.	
	2nd		Bn relieved in the Trenches by 8th York & Lancaster Regt. Bn went back to billets at FLEURBAIX.	
	3rd 4th 5th		Bn in Bde reserve. Weather turned very cold.	
	6th		Bn went into Trenches & relieved 8th Y&L Regt. A very quiet night owing probably to the state of the weather.	
	7th		Quiet day in the Trenches. Enemy shelled CROIX MARECHAL during the afternoon.	
	8th		Enemy very quiet day & night. CONVENT WALL was shelled about 11 am. CASUALTIES: 2 O.R. wounded.	
	9th		Rather more shelling than usual but most of it seemed to be well behind our lines. CASUALTIES: 1 O.R. killed, 2 wounded.	
	10th		In the evening the Bn was relieved by the 2nd Y&L, Bn going back into billets at FLEURBAIX.	

WAR DIARY or INTELLIGENCE SUMMARY

Army Form C. 2118

(Erase heading not required.)

Place	Date	Hour	Summary of Events and Information	Remarks and references to Appendices
	11th		Bn in Billets at FLEURBAIX. CASUALTIES: 1 O.R. wounded.	
	12th		Two Battalions of the 116th Infantry Brigade came into FLEURBAIX & were attached for instruction to the 70th Brigade. Two Coys of the 11th Royal Sussex were attached to this Bn also the Bn 2nd in Command. The other Regt were attached to this Bn. Half Bn of the 11th Royal Sussex Regt & Bn Head HQrs went into trenches in the evening & were attached to the 8th Y & L Regt.	
	13th		A very clear & bright day. In the afternoon FLEURBAIX was heavily shelled. Billets occupied by "A" Coy of this Bn & 2 Machine Gun platoons of the 11th Royal Sussex Regt had large number of shells put into it. The casualties of the two Regts together amounted to 31. CASUALTIES (9 Y & L) 1 Officer wounded, 4 O.R. killed, 9 O.R. wounded.	
	14th		The Bn & 2 Coys of the 11th Royal Sussex Regt went into trenches & relieved the 8th Y & L Regt. There was much more infantry fire than usual during the night. CASUALTIES: 2 O.R. wounded.	
	15th		Our aeroplanes & artillery were very active all the afternoon. In reply BASSETT HOUSE, FLEURBAIX, & LA BOUTILLERIE were shelled. BASSETT HOUSE was set on fire & burned to the ground. CASUALTIES: 1 O.R. killed, 2 O.R. wounded.	

Army Form C. 2118

WAR DIARY
or
INTELLIGENCE SUMMARY

(Erase heading not required.)

Instructions regarding War Diaries and Intelligence Summaries are contained in F.S. Regs., Part II. and the Staff Manual respectively. Title Pages will be prepared in manuscript.

Place	Date	Hour	Summary of Events and Information	Remarks and references to Appendices
	16th		Quiet day. Enemy sent several shells in the direction of FLEURBAIX during the morning. CASUALTIES: 1 O.R. wounded.	
	17th		At 4 p.m. our 8" Howitzers bombarded TURK POINT. 11 rounds were fired & the visible target knocked in 3 places. In retaliation enemy opened a short & vigorous bombardment on CONVENT WALL & our front line. Their shooting was very erratic, no damage was done & no casualties sustained. CASUALTIES: 1 O.R. killed, 2 O.R. wounded.	
	18th		Quiet day in the trenches. In the evening we were relieved by 8th Y & L. The Bn going back to billets in FLEURBAIX.	
	19th		Quiet day in billets.	
	20th		The Brigade were relieved by the 116th Bde & went back into Divl Reserve about SAILLY. The 2 Coys of the 11th Royal Sussex Regt attached to this Bn went into trenches in the evening & joined up with the 2 Coys that had been attached to the 8th Y & L thereby taking over the front line of trenches. This Bn was relieved in billets by the 14th Hants Regt.	

Army Form C. 2118

WAR DIARY
or
INTELLIGENCE SUMMARY
(Erase heading not required.)

Instructions regarding War Diaries and Intelligence Summaries are contained in F. S. Regs., Part II. and the Staff Manual respectively. Title Pages will be prepared in manuscript.

Place	Date MARCH	Hour	Summary of Events and Information	Remarks and references to Appendices
	21st		Bn in Divisional Reserve.	
	22nd			
	23rd			
	24th			
	25th		Preparation being made for move.	
	26th		The Bn marched to the CALONNE AREA in readiness to entrain at MERVILLE. The Bn arrived at CALONNE about 4pm. & went into billet.	
	27th		Bn paraded at 1.30am. & at 2am. marched to MERVILLE STATION. Bn entrained & journeyed to the south of AMIENS & detained at 2pm. Bn then marched via AMIENS to VIGNACOURT where billets were awaiting us. The remainder of the 70th Brigade was billeted in the same village, also Brigade Hdqtrs. Divisional HQs had moved to FLESSELLES.	
	28th		Bn rested in billets at VIGNACOURT	
	29th			
	30th		Bn together with the 11th Sherwood Foresters marched to ST GRATIEN	Brigade Headquarters & French Mortar batteries the whole column been under the command of Lt Col Addison

Army Form C. 2118

WAR DIARY
or
INTELLIGENCE SUMMARY
(Erase heading not required.)

Place	Date	Hour	Summary of Events and Information	Remarks and references to Appendices
	MARCH			
	30th		Leaving MIGNACOURT at 8 am. BN arrived at ST. GRATIEN about 12.30pm. in billets there. The remainder of the Brigade marched the next day under the command of Lt. Col. Humphry D.S.O. Bn together with 11th Sherwood Foresters marched via QUERRIEU & LA HOUSSOYE to billets in ALBERT. Remainder of Brigade marched in on following day.	

SUMMARY OF CASUALTIES DURING MONTH.

1 Officer wounded: Lt. J. S. Thompson

KILLED
11269 Hope J. Ballin
11250 Bgle L. Stroke
18645 Pte A. Carrall
15293 " J. Cooper
18809 " A. V. Graton
4769 " E. L. Evans
16960 " A. Stone

WOUNDED
19041 Pte Fitzwilliam J.   15328 Pte A. Parsons
16855 " R. Bennett   15336 " B. Tebbs
18912 " T. Bensworth   19195 " O. David
11910 " J. Reid   18862 " E. L. Walton
16182 " A. E. Bryers   3867 " Holt. W. H.
15312 " R. G. Clarke   16335 " T. Waller
15038 " Sgt. B. Bowen   10639 " B. Johnson
15611 " L/Cpl G. Bean   19076 " E. Weedin
18982 " Pte G. Bennett   16252 " Hope Daniel
16990 " " T. Kirkwood   15037 Pte T. White
8943 " Pte J. J. Cranely

J. Wilson
Lt. Col.
Comdg. 9th Bn York & Lancaster Regt.

Army Form C. 2118

WAR DIARY
or
INTELLIGENCE SUMMARY
(Erase heading not required.)

Place	Date	Hour	Summary of Events and Information	Remarks and references to Appendices
ALBERT	April 1916.			
	1st		The Battalion took over Trenches X.7/10 to X.13/1 from the 15th Highland Light Infantry. Three Companies were in the firing line & one company in reserve. The 11th Sherwood Foresters took over the trenches on our immediate left. On our right were the 2nd Manchester Regt. belonging to the 32nd Divn. The 8th Bn. York & Lancaster Regt. & the 8th Bn. K.O.Y.L.I. marched into ALBERT during the afternoon & became battalions in Brigade Reserve.	
	2nd		There was a good deal of shrapnel fire & some rifle grenades were fired into our trenches during the night. CASUALTIES: 1 O.R. wounded.	
	3rd		A quiet day, but considerable amount of aerial activity. At different times during the day shrapnel was fired along our communication trenches in the front line. Considerable opportunity seemed to exist for the observation of movement behind the enemy.	

WAR DIARY
or
INTELLIGENCE SUMMARY
(Erase heading not required.)

Army Form C. 2118

Place	Date	Hour	Summary of Events and Information	Remarks and references to Appendices
	Apl 3rd		Lines especially from our left company which occupied trenches sticking downwards from the TARA RIDGE & giving a clear view right across the enemy's position. Several working parties were seen during the day on enemy's 2nd & 3rd lines. CASUALTIES: 1 O.R. killed; 1 O.R. wounded. There was considerable enemy movement on the OVILLERS – LA BOISELLE ROAD this day.	
	4th		Apparently a quiet day. The enemy shelled our Fort Line & Communication Trenches with shrapnel & a few whizz-bangs. They previously ceased and fire on our guns firing on them. There was some aeroplane activity on our front during the morning. Towards evening the enemy's machine gun fire became more high and evident & more accurate. CASUALTIES: 1 O.R. killed, 6 O.R. wounded.	
	5th		A very quiet day; practically no hostility from either side. Enemy apparently to be doing a lot of work on his trenches & keeps his wire apparently in good repair. CASUALTIES: 1 O.R. wounded.	

Army Form C. 2118

WAR DIARY
or
INTELLIGENCE SUMMARY
(Erase heading not required.)

Place	Date	Hour	Summary of Events and Information	Remarks and references to Appendices
	April 6th		Our artillery was fairly active throughout the day shelling the enemy's front line. We also fired rifle grenades in retaliation. Apart from dropping a few shells of small calibre on our communication trenches the enemy was not enterprising at <s>artillery</s>. Many enemy working parties were seen in rear of his lines.	
	7th		Except for the use of rifle grenades on both sides the day was quiet. In this part of the country the enemy is often seen moving in rear of his lines & since taking over this front many German officers have been observed observing our lines.	
	8th		Our artillery shelled the hostile trench a little. During the previous 24 hours the enemy had done much work to his trenches & wire several working parties were observed coming towards the enemy front line. In the evening we were relieved by the 8th Bn. Y. & L. Regt & proceeded to ALBERT & went into Brigade Reserve.	
	9th 10th 11th 12th 13th		Battalion in Brigade Reserve. Apart from perhaps six shells per day	

Army Form C. 2118

WAR DIARY
or
INTELLIGENCE SUMMARY
(Erase heading not required.)

Instructions regarding War Diaries and Intelligence Summaries are contained in F. S. Regs., Part II. and the Staff Manual respectively. Title Pages will be prepared in manuscript.

Place	Date	Hour	Summary of Events and Information	Remarks and references to Appendices
ALBERT	April 14th		Fired in the direction of the Church nothing of note happened on the 11th Inst. A S.O.S message was received in the evening from the Royal Irish Rifles of the Right Brigade. Apart from standing to for some four hours we were not affected by that alarm.	
	15th		We relieved the 8th K.O.Y.L.I. as left Bn in the Brigade, "B" & "C" Coys being in the front line, "D" Coy in Close support & "A" Coy in b Hmphft & was guides successful Reserve. This relief took place in the afternoon & was guides successful Reserve. This relief took place in the afternoon & was guides successful Reserve & 8th K.O.Y.L.I marched into ALBERT & became battalion in reserve. Apart from the fact that the enemy were capable from their position of bringing reverse fires to bear upon us & also enfilade fire everything was very quiet.	
	16th		During the morning some rifle grenades were exchanged. In the evening enemy used machine guns rather freely. About 5 p.m. four shells dropped	

Army Form C. 2118

WAR DIARY
or
INTELLIGENCE SUMMARY
(Erase heading not required.)

Instructions regarding War Diaries and Intelligence Summaries are contained in F.S. Regs., Part II. and the Staff Manual respectively. Title Pages will be prepared in manuscript.

Place	Date	Hour	Summary of Events and Information	Remarks and references to Appendices
	4/6/16		Close to Bn HQs, one – a Direct hit on a new gun pit finished that afternoon. CASUALTIES: 1 O.R. wounded	
	17th		Apparently a quiet day except for a few shells and for a few minor mortars fired on the left company which did no damage. In the afternoon we were relieved by the 2nd Leinster Rifles & marched into Divisional Reserve at HENENCOURT WOOD where we took over their camp. Owing to the bad weather the sick rate was very bad & except this, rain did not lead to improve matters. CASUALTY: 1 O.R. wounded.	
	18th to 24th		Bn still in Divisional Reserve. Training was carried on but under bad conditions owing to the excessive wet & mud prevailing during this period.	

Army Form C. 2118

WAR DIARY
or
INTELLIGENCE SUMMARY
(Erase heading not required.)

Place	Date	Hour	Summary of Events and Information	Remarks and references to Appendices
	25th APRIL		Period in Divisional Reserve over. The Battalion moved into ALBERT as Left Reserve Battalion - Right Sector. The movement was carried out during the evening of this day. The 8th Bn Y & L Regt was the Left Battalion - Right Sector in the line.	
	26th 27th 28th		The Bn still in Brigade Reserve, nothing of any consequence taking place.	
	29th		The Battalion we were supporting was fairly heavily shelled, some of our working parties being up in the Front line at the time. No damage was done either to ours or the 8th Y&L Regt.	From 4am 11.5am & 3.30am
	30th		The day was quiet but towards evening the Right Section was again subject to heavy shelling by the enemy. Both Front, supporting & Communication Trenches came under a heavy fire. The Bn was ordered to "stand to" at about 6pm, about which time the enemy had in addition their range and a desultory fire was	

Army Form C. 2118.

WAR DIARY
or
INTELLIGENCE SUMMARY.
(Erase heading not required.)

Place	Date	Hour	Summary of Events and Information	Remarks and references to Appendices
	April		kept up on our area for about an hour afterwards nothing followed the shelling of the front line & about 10 pm the Battalion received the "Revert to finial" from the Brigade. CASUALTIES: 2 O.R. wounded.	

Wilson Lt Col.
Cdg 9th Bn York & Lancaster Regt.

Army Form C. 2118.

WAR DIARY
or
INTELLIGENCE SUMMARY
(Erase heading not required.)

9th Yorks & Lancs
Vol 6
VIII

Place	Date	Hour	Summary of Events and Information	Remarks and references to Appendices
			ADDENDA TO APRIL.	
			AWARDS	
			On the 18th April the following wire was received from Brigade Headquarters:- "Commander-in-Chief awards Military Medal to 15367 Pte WILLIAM HEAFIELD. AAA. Military Authority, 3rd Corps Message A 698 of 18th." your unit.	
			On the 22nd April the following appeared in 8th Divisional Routine Orders No 401.	
			"The Commander-in-Chief has awarded the Military Medal to No 15662 Hayes 26. Alguith, 9th (Service) Bn York & Lancaster Regt, for the following act of gallantry:- "Near ALBERT between the 1st & 5th April 1916, has shown continuous courage & coolness in patrol work. As N.C.O. permanently in charge of his Company this N.C.O. was doing fairly fft Alguith has done consistently good work. On the 6th April whilst employed among forty unfortunately wounded in the thigh on the right of the in erecting wire in NO MAN'S LAND."	

Army Form C. 2118

WAR DIARY
or
INTELLIGENCE SUMMARY
(Erase heading not required.)

Summary of Events and Information

SUMMARY OF CASUALTIES FOR APRIL

Killed.
4757 Pte G. Hallas.
3867 " W. B. Hodder.
15859 " J. Robert.

Wounded.
16822 Pte A. Hall.
18902 " J. W. H. Harding
16927 " J. Hunter.
23114 L/Cpl F. Glew
16714 Pte E. Crossland
19038 " F. Foster
15502 " Waite R.A.
15662 " L/Cpl Asquith H.O.
15410 Pte F. Ellis
15598 " J. Hidden
15955 " J. Barker.

Place	Date	Hour

8th, Division.

70th, Brigade.

9th, York & Lancs.

May, 1916.

To Officer i/c
   Infantry Records,
      York,

Herewith please find Copy of
War Diary for the month of MAY.

W Thomson
2nd Lt & a/Adjt.

WAR DIARY or INTELLIGENCE SUMMARY

Army Form C. 2118

Place	Date MAY	Hour	Summary of Events and Information	Remarks and references to Appendices
TRENCHES	1st		The 18 Battalion relieved the 8th Bn Y & L Regt as left Bn. Right relieving movement commenced at about 6 am by sections. Although a long process it was quite successful. The 8th Bn being finally relieved & moving out before mid-day. The 8th Y & L then marched into ALBERT taking over our billets & becoming our supporting Bn. Apart from a few rifle grenades & heavy mortars the day was quiet. Only two Coys occupied the front line, D Coy on the left & "A" Coy on the right, "B" Coy being in support to "D" & "A". The trenches here are very close together the Right Coys front being in places only about 60 yards away & having about nine craters between themselves & the enemy.	[Marks for Brielle...]
	2nd		A comparatively quiet day. The enemy uses another form of "Bilcau". Here they are a kind of trench mortar & nicknamed through the fact that their shape & appearance suggest such. They are however very demoralising in effect owing to being charged with nothing but high explosive. Each "oileau" weighs about 40 lb. The enemy fires quite accurately & quite a lot of them. He is also very persistent in the use of rifle grenades sending over a great	

WAR DIARY or INTELLIGENCE SUMMARY

Army Form C. 2118

Place	Date	Hour	Summary of Events and Information	Remarks and references to Appendices
	3rd		number. There was not much artillery action. There is a tremendous lot of work to be done in this part of the line & the Bn. is making good improvement to the trenches. CASUALTIES: 1 O.R. wounded. Apart from intermittent shelling the day was comparatively quiet. About 4 p.m. we blew up a mine about Trench K 13. L. 9. 8. which we followed up with a short but heavy bombardment. The reply by the enemy was very feeble. The Germans here make persistent use of the "Minens". In consequence of this we gave them a very lively time with our artillery the volume of which there are certainly diminished the next day. CASUALTIES: Nil.	
	4th		We got the "Heavies" on to one or two points which were suspected the Germans made use of for the firing of Trench Mortars & rifle grenades. The shooting was excellent. Apart from a few trench mortars to which we replied vigorously the day was very quiet. CASUALTIES: 2 O.R. wounded.	

Army Form C. 2118

WAR DIARY
or
INTELLIGENCE SUMMARY
(Erase heading not required.)

Instructions regarding War Diaries and Intelligence Summaries are contained in F. S. Regs., Part II. and the Staff Manual respectively. Title Pages will be prepared in manuscript.

Place	Date MAY.	Hour	Summary of Events and Information	Remarks and references to Appendices
	5th		Comparatively active day for artillery. The enemy bombarded our front line communication trenches & support lines intermittently all day. They also met a great number of rifle grenades, ortans, & trench mortars in accordance with pre-arranged scheme we bombarded the enemy's trenches at midnight doing good firing. The enemy retaliated vigorously using against us shells of fairly large calibre. Our Right Company's telephone communication was cut during this but excellent communication was kept up between the Coy & Bn HQRS by means of a signalling lamp placed in the front line in case of emergency. Like this, some days before, judging from explosions which took place in the enemy's trench it is assumed that we did him some little damage. CASUALTIES. 1 O.R. killed, 4 O.R. wounded.	
	6th		A quiet day the artillery being especially so. A few rifle grenades & trench mortars were however fired into our trenches. During the past week the enemy has been very daring in the use of auto aircraft several of our machines have flown low over his lines the only retaliation being rifle & M.G. fire. CASUALTIES. 3 O.R. wounded.	

1375 Wt. W593/826 1,000,000 4/15 J.B.C. & A. A.D.S.S./Forms/C. 2118.

Army Form C. 2118

WAR DIARY
or
INTELLIGENCE SUMMARY
(Erase heading not required.)

Instructions regarding War Diaries and Intelligence Summaries are contained in F.S. Regs., Part II. and the Staff Manual respectively. Title Pages will be prepared in manuscript.

Place	Date MAY	Hour	Summary of Events and Information	Remarks and references to Appendices
	7th		Another fairly quiet day. The enemy fired some 80 rifle grenades into our line besides trench mortars. His rifle grenade fire was quite good, some landing into trenches 600 yards from his position with wonderful accuracy. Our 8" How: registered on LA BOISSELLE with a view to carry out a systematic bombardment, but as the day was cloudy our aeroplanes could not have been able to observe correctly, & the proceedings were postponed.	
	8th		We had hoped to carry out a systematic bombardment but as the day was cloudy our aeroplanes could not have been able to observe correctly, & the proceedings were postponed. The got very much shelling. Our 8" How. bombarded LA BOISSELLE. The enemy replied to this fairly vigorously. He was however fairly persistent with rifle grenade fire, firing one a distance of over 600 yards. The enemy appears to do most of his "strafing" here from WYE SAP a place which is constantly fired on by our artillery with comparatively little effect. CASUALTIES: 2 O.R. wounded.	
	9th		Comparatively active day. The enemy's artillery & trench mortars doing some little damage to our trenches. Our artillery acted promptly & retaliated more especially on the ever famous WYE SAP. We also	

WAR DIARY
or
INTELLIGENCE SUMMARY
(Erase heading not required.)

Place	Date MAY	Hour	Summary of Events and Information	Remarks and references to Appendices
	10th		made use of Trench Mortars & Rifle Grenades. A lively day for artillery, the enemy shelling our front line, communication & support lines intermittently throughout the day with guns both of small & large calibre. We also fired trench mortars in salvoes doing some damage to our trenches last night. Our artillery retaliated many times & as usual WYE SAP came in for its fair share, but at the end of all this the men in the top felt over the last shot - a Trench Mortar.	
	11th		Battalion on our left made a raid in the early morning. The centre of our front was not shelled but both flanks were heavily shelled & a heavy barrage was set up. The enemy replied not vigorously to our fire but considering the number of shells sent over the damage to our trenches was not great & our casualties consisted of one man slightly hit in the cheek. After 11 days in the trenches we were relieved on this day by the 26th Northumberland Fusiliers. The relief taking place by daylight in the early morning	

WAR DIARY
or
INTELLIGENCE SUMMARY
(Erase heading not required.)

Army Form C. 2118

Place	Date	Hour	Summary of Events and Information	Remarks and references to Appendices
HENENCOURT	May 12th		I was quite successful. The Bn proceeded into Divisional Reserve at HENENCOURT WOOD arriving here about 10 am. The stay in the Trenches was the longest the Battalion has had in the Trenches & although the men were naturally very tired & worn the Bn throughout the period did itself the utmost credit. CASUALTIES: 2 O.R. wounded.	
	13th to 18th		The day was devoted to interior economy. A special raiding party of 2 officers & 60 O.R. was formed & it is intended to train them in the many arts of raiding from now onwards. Bn still in Divisional Reserve, a systematic programme of training being carried out.	
	19th		The Brigade moved forward to a more forward area in Divisional Reserve. This Battalion moved into No 5 Camp. HENENCOURT WOOD & the remaining Battalions moved up into MILLENCOURT.	
	21 & 22nd		Training still continued.	

Army Form C. 2118.

WAR DIARY
or
INTELLIGENCE SUMMARY
(Erase heading not required.)

Instructions regarding War Diaries and Intelligence Summaries are contained in F. S. Regs., Part II. and the Staff Manual respectively. Title Pages will be prepared in manuscript.

Place	Date MAY	Hour	Summary of Events and Information	Remarks and references to Appendices
	22nd		300 men & 7 Officers of the Battalion went on a working party, digging a new communication trench. The following is a report sent by the B.R.E. to the Headquarters, 70th Brigade.:- C.R.E. 855. 23.5.16 H.Q. 70th Inf. Bde. "The 300 men of 9th Y.L. did a remarkably fine piece of digging on the new PORT LOUIS on 21/22 (night). I have seldom seen better. Each man did about 70 c.ft in dark in 4 hours."	
	23rd to 26th		Bn still in Divisional Reserve carrying out programme of training & supplying working parties.	
	27th		The Brigade moved forward into the line taking over the Left Section of the 8th Div Front. His Bn was in Brigade Reserve to the 8th Bn Y.L. Regt in the Left Sub Section of the Brigade Section.	

Army Form C. 2118

WAR DIARY
or
INTELLIGENCE SUMMARY

(Erase heading not required.)

Instructions regarding War Diaries and Intelligence Summaries are contained in F. S. Regs., Part II. and the Staff Manual respectively. Title Pages will be prepared in manuscript.

Place	Date	Hour	Summary of Events and Information	Remarks and references to Appendices
ALBERT	May 28th 31st		The Battalion still in Brigade Reserve. There was very little shelling of ALBERT & only on one occasion did any shells fall near our billets.	

WAR DIARY
or
INTELLIGENCE SUMMARY

(Erase heading not required.)

Place	Date	Hour	Summary of Events and Information	Remarks and references to Appendices

			AWARDS.
			
			On the 15th inst the following appeared in 3rd Divisional Routine Orders No 499:-
			
			The Commander-in-Chief has awarded Military Medal to the under-mentioned men for the following act of gallantry:-
			
			   No 9905 Pte G. Brannan, 9th Bn York & Lancaster Regt;
			   No 14866 " J. T. Woodcock do
			
			"On the night of the 5th/6th May 1916, in the trenches in front of ALBERT during a bombardment, the telephone wires to the right Coy Advanced HQrs were cut by shell fire, the Company 2nd in Command who was at that point, required to send an important message to Bn HQrs. Ptes Brannan & Woodcock, who had just returned from putting up barbed wire volunteered to take this message. They were successful in doing so in spite of the fact that the trenches through which they had to pass were being very heavily shelled	

Place	Date	Hour	Summary of Events and Information	Remarks and references to Appendices
			with high explosives & shrapnel at the time. They also succeeded in taking a reply message back to Company Advanced Headquarters, the distance each way being about 1800 yds. The names of these two men have been brought to notice previously on several occasions for good work done as permanent wiring party."	

WAR DIARY
or
INTELLIGENCE SUMMARY

(Erase heading not required.)

Army Form C. 2118

Summary of Events and Information

CASUALTIES DURING THE MONTH.

KILLED.

No 19196 Pte W. Greenaway.
" 12901 " L. Johnson.

WOUNDED

No 16579 Pte J.T. Rill.
 " 8677   " Hylde Osborn.
 " 18966 " W. Grayson
 " 19160 " F. Plumfield
 " 19163 " E.E. Rutter
 " 13289 " J. Kirby
 " 19057 " E. Hall
 " 16123 " J. Bowyer
 " 16154 " Hodkinson
 " 8771   " J.E. Guy
 " 8879   " J.H. Longley
 " 9376   " J.H. Longley
 " 19103 " R. Richardson
 " 3906   " R. Bernshaw
 " 12793 " J. Williams
 " 15353 " P. Weltman
 " 16135 " E. Loosemore

Mathews Lt Col.
Bdg 9th Bn York & Lancaster Regt.

8th, Division.

70th, Brigade.

9th, York & Lancs.

June , 1916.

WAR DIARY
or
INTELLIGENCE SUMMARY VII

Army Form C. 2118.

Place	Date JUNE	Hour	Summary of Events and Information	Remarks and references to Appendices
ALBERT DISTRICT	1st		The Battalion relieved the 8th Bn. York & Lancaster Regt in the left sub sector. The relief was carried out during daylight commencing at noon & was successful. There was much artillery activity on both sides & at 8 & at 11 usual the War received a large share of the hostile retaliation. Considerable damage was done to WALTNEY STREET & the mouth of a mine shaft was blown in. During the night several officers patrols investigated NO MAN'S LAND. All the patrols were considerably hampered by hostile machine gun fire. Chapnel & 77mm shells. The enemy frequently had no patrols out this night. They continually swept our lines with machine guns. One man on patrol was struck in the head. His steel helmet in all probability saving his life. CASUALTIES. 2.OR wounded.	
	2nd		The day was again chiefly devoted to much shelling. The enemy's machine guns were not so active as on the previous day. A number of shells passed well overhead going in the direction of AVELUY & ALBERT. CASUALTIES: 1 Officer wounded. 11 OR wounded.	

WAR DIARY
or
INTELLIGENCE SUMMARY

Army Form C. 2118

Place	Date	Hour	Summary of Events and Information	Remarks and references to Appendices
	JUNE 3rd		During the morning our artillery shelled OVILLERS & LA BOISELLE. Machine guns were active all day, the enemy retaliating with vigour. At 11.30pm a heavy bombardment commenced on our left & was kept up for 2½ hours. After about an hour the enemy opened rapid rifle fire on our trenches. I sent up many Very lights. This happened just after one of our patrols had returned.	
	4th		The Bn was relieved by the 2nd Bn West Yorkshire Regt & went into Divisional Reserve at HENNENCOURT WOOD. During our tour in the Trenches a large number of Officers patrols went out gained much valuable information regarding NO MAN'S LAND. The Bn arrived at HENNENCOURT WOOD about 5pm & after bivouacing in the wood for about three hours took over No 5 Camp from the 2nd Bn Royal Irish Rifles. CASUALTIES. 2. O.R. wounded.	

WAR DIARY
or
INTELLIGENCE SUMMARY
(Erase heading not required.)

Army Form C. 2118

Place	Date	Hour	Summary of Events and Information	Remarks and references to Appendices
	JUNE 5th/6/12th		The Battalion still in Divisional Reserve. An excellent programme of training was carried out. On three days the Battalion visited the FRANVILLERS Training area where the attack was practised. On one occasion aeroplanes co-operated of the signalling of our Battalion signallers was reported to be "Good". The inclement weather interfered with operations but much miniature work was done.	
	12th		After spending the day at FRANVILLERS the Battalion relieved the 2nd Bn Royal Berkshire Regt in the MILLENCOURT area, taking over billets in MILLENCOURT which were not very satisfactory.	
	13th 14th 15th 16,18th		Bn still at MILLENCOURT. A large number of working parties were provided for the front line & posts & classes were also continued.	

WAR DIARY
or
INTELLIGENCE SUMMARY

(Erase heading not required.)

Army Form C. 2118.

Place	Date June	Hour	Summary of Events and Information	Remarks and references to Appendices
	19.		The Bn relieved the 8th Y.R. Regt in the Left Sector of the Divisional Front. The movement began about 10.0pm. & was completed just about 2.30 am. The remainder of the night was very quiet. Judging from the cheerfulness of the men the time spent in Divisional Reserve had done them a lot of good.	
	20.		Except for spasmodic salvoes at odd intervals on our front line trenches of the left Coy & a few rifle grenades, the enemy was very quiet. Preparing for future operations our guns were more or less active in registration, a fact which did not seem to rouse the enemy's enthusiasm to retaliation fire. The enemy at the Cross Roads in NO MANS LAND of the left Coy had been giving rather a lot of trouble lately. The Right Flank Trench Mortar Officer of the Brigade & a patrol under the Right Flank Trench Mortar Officer of the Brigade which included one of our machine gun detachment went out with the object of annihilating the offenders. The scheme was an excellent j.....try, being killed, two of the detachment being wounded & some of the Trench mortar men were also wounded. The enemy was not encountered	

Army Form C. 2118.

WAR DIARY
or
INTELLIGENCE SUMMARY
(Erase heading not required.)

Instructions regarding War Diaries and Intelligence Summaries are contained in F. S. Regs., Part II. and the Staff Manual respectively. Title Pages will be prepared in manuscript.

Place	Date JUNE	Hour	Summary of Events and Information	Remarks and references to Appendices
	21st		sent he found a most excellent site with his Lewis Gun from the front line for dealing with our patrol. The enemys artillery registered on & about the left Bay's communication trench rather more active in the evening. The R.N. settle rifles were very active during this tour on the trenches getting ready the Assembly dug-out stores for ammunition, R.E. material etc. The men worked with much enthusiasm. Throughout the day our guns continued their programme of registration & one began to appreciate that "all things were moving" as the expression goes. CAPT. W. PRITCHARD reports he was very busy during this tour on the trenches getting ready the Assembly dug-out stores for ammunition, R.E. material etc. The men worked with much enthusiasm.	
	22nd		The enemys retaliation for our registration was becoming heavier & ranging from the ridge overhead he was enfilading in some counter battery work. Our artillery was fairly busy, our trenches dropping shells on the enemys 2nd & 3rd line. In the early morning our	

2449 Wt. W14957/M90 750,000 1/16 J.B.C. & A. Forms/C.2118/12.

Army Form C. 2118.

WAR DIARY
or
INTELLIGENCE SUMMARY
(Erase heading not required.)

Place	Date	Hour	Summary of Events and Information	Remarks and references to Appendices
	23rd		Anti-aircraft guns brought down an enemy aeroplane in the enemy's lines. Our roving parties had done good work in thinning out wire preparatory to future operations. Apart from continued registration the day was comparatively quiet. The Bn was relieved by the 8th K.O.Y.L.I. & marched back to TYLERS REDOUBT to await orders for the advance. Whether the closeness of the night or what, the relief was not a success from the time point of view, the relief taking some six or seven hours. In spite of the flying conditions such as rain, mud, etc, the men was comparatively cheerful on its arrival at TYLERS REDOUBT. The operation this day were rather expensive to us T. Day being the full day of the long-thought-of great advance. The bombardment was to start on this night that owing to the fact that so many regts were on the move it was not a success with the wagons originally intended.	

WAR DIARY
or
INTELLIGENCE SUMMARY

Army Form C. 2118.

Place	Date JUNE	Hour	Summary of Events and Information	Remarks and references to Appendices
	24th		U DAY. The RA spent a quiet day in TYLERS REDOUBT. The bombardment increased. The 18 pdr batteries indulged in wire cutting. The Heavies went in for counter battery work whilst the 9.2 & 12 inch guns registered on FLERS & LA SARS. Machine Guns co-operated with artillery at night to prevent the enemy from repairing his wire. All outstanding registration by guns were completed. The effect on the German is not known but it is assumed that a certain amount of damage was caused.	
	25th		V. DAY. Another quiet day for the RA in TYLERS REDOUBT. Wire cutting & bombardment with all guns took place & more counter battery work was done. The Corps Heavy Guns concentrated their fire suddenly on various points & villages in rear of the German line. The highest rate of fire was opened at a given time, the time varying from 5 to 12 minutes. The places so deluged such treatment were POZIÈRES, CONTALMAISON, BAZENTIN LE PETIT, & BAZENTIN. The special bombardment to be carried out from	

WAR DIARY or INTELLIGENCE SUMMARY

Army Form C. 2118.

Place	Date	Hour	Summary of Events and Information	Remarks and references to Appendices
	26th		to ZERO on Z Day was also indulged in, i.e. artillery was concentrated on all the German lines working front 15 rear & lifting as one gun. During the night Bosche worked in conjunction with the Germans artillery to prevent the both Bosche repairing his damaged wire. W Day. Our Battalion still engaged in act and also the regions of Beech in TYLERS REDOUBT. In general the work of the artillery was as yesterday special attention being paid to the railway loop at donte west end of MARTINPUICH. The various lines of the German trenches were subjected to the intense bombardment which will take place at the ZERO HOUR on Z day. Smoke was discharged along the front at various intervals commencing early morning. The Coys working on our left & right discharged gas during east of their demonstrations. As yesterday the effect of this is not known from the German about front, but from various rumours it is suggested its was not received with	

Army Form C. 2118.

WAR DIARY
or
INTELLIGENCE SUMMARY
(Erase heading not required.)

Instructions regarding War Diaries and Intelligence Summaries are contained in F.S. Regs., Part II. and the Staff Manual respectively. Title Pages will be prepared in manuscript.

Place	Date	Hour	Summary of Events and Information	Remarks and references to Appendices
	27.		good price. The 25th Brigade carried out a raid killing some 50 Germans & bringing in one much wounded prisoner. He stated that the Germans expected small raids but nothing in the event of a general offensive. The division on our left had many casualties some over to them & after receiving their gas over others were caught by the intense Shrapnel barrage set up. X Day. Run as yesterday. The work of the artillery was also as yesterday special attention being paid to his rearward lines & at 10.0 p.m. in the evening the bombardment was very intense indeed. Gas was liberated on our Divisional front in the early morning & it is hoped with good effect. Smoke was as yesterday, liberated at odd intervals. The general opinion is that the German reply to our bombardment was not great although large guns were suspected in the vicinity.	

WAR DIARY
or
INTELLIGENCE SUMMARY

Army Form C. 2118.

Place	Date	Hour	Summary of Events and Information	Remarks and references to Appendices
	JUNE 28.		**Y DAY.** The Battalion was in orders to move forward tomorrow, the evening of this day, but it is presumed owing chiefly to the bad weather which has prevailed during the last two days this order was cancelled. In general the bombardment carried out by our artillery was as on the last two previous days. Special attention being paid to wire cutting & the bombardment of the enemy's lines. From reports it would appear that the German retaliation although heavy & concentrated on certain parts of the line such as STANLEY & CHORLEY STREETS was not - taking into consideration the whole of the Divisional Front - more than a normal supply of guns could effect in contra-distribution to preparation made in view of an expected bombardment prior to an offensive attack. When our concentrated bombardment took place on the enemy's first line, firing from the large number of red lights sent up & assuming seek to be the signal for retaliation the Germans infantry was certainly not satisfied with the way his own guns retaliated on our lines. Some shells were dropped into BEAUCOURT 1 mile from where we were & by Lens Fusilade.	

WAR DIARY
or
INTELLIGENCE SUMMARY

(Erase heading not required.)

Army Form C.

Place	Date June	Hour	Summary of Events and Information	Remarks and references to Appendices
	29th		The Battalion still in TYLERS REDOUBT awaiting orders to move into the forward Area (Orders came to send forward parties for 2 days on 28th inst.)	
	19th 30th		Orders received that the Bn had to move forward into the forward Area, and the Bn moved from TYLERS REDOUBT to the place of assembly in the forward Area to take shelter the Arsault. About 30 men were left behind in Reserve in LONE VALLEY under the command of Major J.S. ARMSTRONG, also the Officers named below Capt F.J. Bosser 2nd Lt. A.L. Price " " F.D. Howe " " R.R.L. Brown.	
	1/2 July		The Bn marched to the trenches without a casualty. During the night a very heavy bombardment from Liege. The enemy retaliated on our front line. The weather was fine and the ground dry. N wind.	
			Strength of Bn going into action. 25 Offrs. 736 O.R.	
			Casualties during march. 1 Officer Killed in action. 23 O.R's	

J. Armstrong Major.
Comg 9th Bn. York Lancaster Regt.

70th Inf.Bde.
23rd Div.

Battn. with Bde.
rejoined from
8th Div. 17.7.16.

9th BATTN. THE YORK & LANCASTER REGIMENT.

J U L Y

1 9 1 6

Attached:

Appendices.

WAR DIARY
INTELLIGENCE SUMMARY

(Erase heading not required.)

Army Form C. 2118.

23/7 9 Yorkshires Vol 8

Place	Date	Hour	Summary of Events and Information	Remarks and references to Appendices
9 Yorkshires	1916 JULY 1st		On the 1st July the Bn. was in action. Nothing official as regards the casualties could be ascertained. C.O. reported wounded (unofficial). Major Lewis reported killed (unofficial). Adjt. Lt. McCallum reported wounded (official). Orders received that the Bn. was being relieved. About 7 p.m. arrangements being made for the comfort of the men who returned safely out of action. G.S. Wagons & Limbers were sent patrolling the roads between Long Valley & Crucifix Corner under orders to pick up any men who were on their way to rejoin the Bn. in Long Valley. 180 returned up to 10 p.m. Strength of Bn. going into action, 25 Officers, 736 other ranks.	
	2nd		3 Officers & 180 men rejoined the Bn. from action during the early morning. The Officers included Capt. W.V. Price, 2nd Lt. S.R. to Staples, & 2nd Lt. S.K. Bence. Capt. E.V. Price & 2nd Lt. S.R. to Staples unhurt. 2nd Lt. S.K. Bence slight bruise on left shoulder. About 3 p.m. orders were received that the Bn. had to entrain at DERNANCOURT STATION. The Bn. paraded in LONG VALLEY at 10.15 p.m. & marched to DERNANCOURT STATION.	

Army Form C. 2118.

WAR DIARY
~~INTELLIGENCE SUMMARY~~
(Erase heading not required.)

Instructions regarding War Diaries and Intelligence Summaries are contained in F. S. Regs., Part II. and the Staff Manual respectively. Title Pages will be prepared in manuscript.

Place	Date JULY	Hour	Summary of Events and Information	Remarks and references to Appendices
	3rd.		arriving here at 1.15 a.m. H.Q's party and two coys. entrained at 5 a.m., the remainder of the Bn. at 9 a.m. The transport proceeded by road to ARGOUVES.	
	4th.		The Bn. bivouaced at ARGOUVES for the night.	
			The Bn. marched from ARGOUVES to OISSY and arrived in billets at OISSY at 4.30 p.m. — a very interesting march. The weather was very close.	
	5th.		The Bn. still in billets at OISSY. Part of the day was devoted to interior Economy, and a parade took place at 4 p.m. when General Gordon inspected the men and congratulated them on their success during the recent fighting which they had been through at OVILLERS and NAB ESC. At 10 p.m. orders were received from Divisional H.Q's. that the 10th Brigade would entrain for (destination not known) on the 6th instant.	
	6th		The Bn. marched from billets at OISSY to SALEUX STN. where they entrained, marching via BOVELLES, GURGNEMICOURT. Time proposed to entrain 7.30 p.m.	

2449 Wt. W14957/M90 750,000 1/16 J.B.C. & A. Forms/C.2118/12.

Army Form C. 2118.

WAR DIARY

INTELLIGENCE SUMMARY

(Erase heading not required.)

Instructions regarding War Diaries and Intelligence Summaries are contained in F. S. Regs, Part II. and the Staff Manual respectively. Title Pages will be prepared in manuscript.

Place	Date JULY	Hour	Summary of Events and Information	Remarks and references to Appendices
	7th		The Bn. detrained at Station & marched to BRUAY, arriving at their billets at 8 a.m. No work was carried out during the day, the men resting. The weather was favourable.	
	8th		The Bn. still in billets.	
	9th		The Bn. still in billets.	
	10th		The Bn. still in billets. During the morning the G.O.C. 8th Division inspected the Bn. & congratulated the men on the work they had recently performed.	
	11th		The Bn. still in billets. The programme of work being composed of Bayonet fighting, Musketry, & training of Lewis Gunners & Bombers.	
	12th		The Bn. still in billets. A Draft of 101 consisting of 57 K.O.S.B., 33 D.L.I., 11 Yorkshire Regt arrived. A small lot of fellows.	
	13th		The G.O.C. Inspected the Draft which arrived yesterday. A Draft of 283 was taken on the strength of Bn. which consisted of 60 Royal Scots, 22 K.O.Y.L.I, 38 W. Yorks, 37 Yorkshire, & 126 E. Yorks	

Army Form C. 2118.

WAR DIARY
INTELLIGENCE SUMMARY
(Erase heading not required.)

Place	Date JULY	Hour	Summary of Events and Information	Remarks and references to Appendices
	14th		The Bn. still in billets. At 2.30 p.m. the Bn. was inspected by the Army Commander.	
	15th		The Bn. still in billets. Orders were received that the Bn. would entrain at HOUDAIN STATION on the 16th instant. During the period in which the Bn. was in billets in BRUAY, a satisfactory programme of work was carried out, i.e. Bayonet fighting, Lewis Gun Course, Instruction to young Officers and N.C.O's, & Instruction in Bombing & Lewis Guns.	
	16th		The Bn. left BRUAY at 10.30 a.m. and marched to HOUDAIN STATION where it entrained and arrived at AMIENS STN. at 8.30 p.m., the Battalion then marched to billets at POULAINVILLE arriving there about 12 midnight.	
	17th		The Bn. left POULAINVILLE at 8.30 am. & marched to PIERREGOT, arriving at their billets there at about 11.30 a.m. In the afternoon General Sir M. Babington (G.O.C. 23rd Division) inspected the Bn.	

WAR DIARY
or
INTELLIGENCE SUMMARY

(Erase heading not required.)

Army Form C. 2118

Place	Date	Hour	Summary of Events and Information	Remarks and references to Appendices
	JULY 18th		The day was devoted to special training. Gas Helmet Drill, Bayonet fighting & Manual Exercises; instruction was also given to Lewis Gunners & Signallers.	
	19th		Programme of work for the day included Gas Helmet Drill, Bayonet fighting, Manual Exercises.	
	20th		A Lecture was held in the afternoon at the Cinematograph Hall, Pierregot, on the new Gas Shell being used by the enemy. About 6 p.m. a wire was received stating that the Brigade would move off at about 9.30 a.m. on the 21st instant, for BAIZEUX WOOD.	
	21st		The Bn. left Pierregot at 9.0 a.m. and marched to BAIZEUX WOOD, arriving there about 1 p.m. - have then	

WAR DIARY
or
INTELLIGENCE SUMMARY
(Erase heading not required.)

Army Form C. 2118

Instructions regarding War Diaries and Intelligence Summaries are contained in F. S. Regs, Part II. and the Staff Manual respectively. Title Pages will be prepared in manuscript.

Place	Date	Hour	Summary of Events and Information	Remarks and references to Appendices
	JULY 22nd		Bn. at Baizeux Wood. In the evening message received from Bde. re holding ourselves in readiness to move off at half an hour's notice.	
	23rd		In the morning the "half-hour's notice" was suspended by wire from Bde. In the afternoon the programme of work consisted of Extended Order Drill and Fire Control.	
	24th		Orders were received that we should move on the morrow.	
	25th		The Bn. left BAIZEUX WOOD at 9 a.m., & marched to SHELTER WOOD, where it relieved the 11th Gloucester-shire Regt about 4.30 p.m. "A" Cos. took up positions in front of Shelter Wood — "A" "B" Co. at the Cutting, "C" "D" at Quadrangle.	
	26th		The Bn. at Shelter Wood and Cos. at above Assembly places. 2nd Lt. Ross sprained his ankle, & 2nd Lt. Fitzgerald reported missing.	

WAR DIARY
INTELLIGENCE SUMMARY
(Erase heading not required.)

Army Form C. 2118

Instructions regarding War Diaries and Intelligence Summaries are contained in F. S. Regs., Part II. and the Staff Manual respectively. Title Pages will be prepared in manuscript.

Place	Date	Hour	Summary of Events and Information	Remarks and references to Appendices
	JULY 27th		The Bn. relieved the 8th Bn. York & Lancs in the front line trench, commencing at 9.0 a.m. "C" Coy occupied the "left front line Coy," "D" Coy the "right front line Coy," "A" Coy the "left second line Coy" & "B" Coy the "right second line Coy". Trenches were deepened & improved, ammunition & bomb stores were made, also Latrines.	
	28th		The artillery, both hostile and our own, was very active during the day. Left front trench extended and deepened. Posts put up for about 30 yards, & some wire.	
	29th	12 midnight & 2 a.m.	During the early hours of the morning — between 12 midnight & 2 a.m. — a very heavy barrage took place. Commencing about 9.0 a.m. the 11th Sherwood Foresters relieved the 9th York & Lancs in the front line trenches, the latter took up the doeventh places of the "Sherwoods" in the road Guieucourt–Contalmaison, Just North of LOZENGE WOOD. 2nd Lt. G. A. Williams, wounded. Capt. A. Hines wounded.	

Army Form C. 2118.

WAR DIARY
or
INTELLIGENCE SUMMARY
(Erase heading not required.)

Place	Date	Hour	Summary of Events and Information	Remarks and references to Appendices
	July 1916 30		The Bn. resting in reserve.	
	31st		The Bn. did in reserve. The lines were cleared, equipment, arms, ammunition found lying about were salvaged. A Working Party of 200 was supplied to work in the *O.G.1. & O.G.2. Support Trenches. During the day we were under Shrapnel fire several times — no casualties. *O.G. = "Old German".	

Casualties for month ending July 31st. 1916:-
Officers = 4
Other Ranks = 56

A.B.Palmer. Major.
Comdg. 9th Bn. York & Lancaster Regt.

APPENDICES.

Operation Order No. 1.

By Lt. Col. A. J. B. Addison
Commanding 9th Bn. York & Lancaster Regt.

Ref ce Map 1-5000.   16-6-16

GENERAL IDEA (1).

In accordance with orders issued by the GHQ 4th Army, III Corps will attack the enemy's position.
The 8th Division will carry out the attack in the following order:- viz: 3 Brigades in line – the 23rd Brigade on the right – the 25th Brigade in the Centre & 70th Brigade on Left.
The flanks of the 70th Brigade will advance by the following points:-

<u>Right</u>- A line drawn through points 11-85-28-62-90-94-40- 30-85-48-91.

<u>Left</u>- A line drawn through points 22-56-12-93-N of 47-N of 81- a point about half way between points 65 & 48.

2.

The 25th Brigade will be operating on our immediate right & the 32nd Division on our left.
The 19 Division being in support to the 8th Division.

(2) ALPHABETICAL LETTERS REPRESENTING DAYS OPERATIONS.
The days of operations are described as: T. U. V. W. X. Y. Z.
T being the first day & Z being the day of assault.

(3) ARTILLERY BOMBARDMENT
An artillery bombardment lasting five days previous to the assault will be carried out, commencing on U day.

(4) R.E. CO-OPERATION
The 2nd Field Coy R.E. will work with the 70 Brigade & will consolidate certain points & trenches in conjunction with the infantry.

(5) TRENCH MORTAR.
Trench Mortar will cover the first assault.

3.

(6) MACHINE GUNS	Scheme for attack, & position of certain points which they will eventually occupy will be issued later.
(7) ATTACK FORMATION.	The 70th Brigade will carry out the attack in the following formation:- 2 Battalions in front line. 1 Battalion in Support. 1 Battalion in Reserve. The first two Battalions will advance in four waves. The Supporting Battalion will cover the whole frontage of the Bde & will advance in two waves. The Reserve Bn will advance in two waves & will consolidate the "1st" position to be consolidated & the "2nd position to be consolidated". Distribution of Battalion is as follows:- Right front line Bn = 8th K.O.Y.L.I. ("A" Bn) Left " " " = 8 Y & L ("B" Bn) Supporting Battalion = 9th Y & L ("C" Bn) Reserve Battalion = 11 Ches: Fus: ("D" Bn) Bns will be referred to as A.B.C.D. Bns in future.

4.

(8) POSITIONS TO BE CONSOLIDATED BY "D" Bn.	First position from point 9/62 on the right to point 32/12. 2nd position from point 33/85 on the right to 33/27.
(9) DIVISIONAL OBJECTIVE.	Divisional objective from 34/91 inclusive through 34/74. 34/65. to about R.28.c.2.0.
(10) ASSEMBLY OF POSITION	Battalions will move into assembly of positions as follows:—

"A" Bn. Front line trenches with its right resting on LONGRIDGE ST. & its left at the sap entrance just north of BAMBERBRIDGE STREET.

"B" Bn. left of A Bn. to a point about 30 yards north of STANLEY STREET.

"C" Bn. 2 boys in QUARRYBRAE. ST.
         1 boy in LIVERPOOL AVENUE
         1 boy in BAMBERBRIDGE. ST.
with the new cut across to front line trench.

"D" Bn. in Reserve.

5.

(11) PATROLS. During the final night of bombardment strong officer patrol will be sent up to the German wire and, if possible, into the German trenches, to see what effect the bombardment has had & how the German line is held.

(12) PREPARATION FOR THE ASSAULT.
GAS

Along the front X.13.b.3.7. to X.1.d.1.0. gas will be liberated as described in APPENDIX "D".

SMOKE. Smoke will be liberated along the whole divisional front for half an hour at 6-26 A.M. on Y day in accordance with instructions contained in APPENDIX "E".
A smoke barrage by trench mortars will also be carried out by the left of the 70th Brigade on the day of assault.

(13) WIRE CUTTING. Starting of the night 16/17th & continued every night our wire will be thinned out so that on the night of Y/Z. the total removal of wire will only

6

be a matter of a few minutes. Care must be taken not to give this operation away.

(14) CONTACT AIR PATROLS. Aeroplanes will work throughout the day as contact patrols. Bns will arrange for flare signals to be lighted at each line of enemy trenches when captured.

(15) On our portion of the line the following communication trenches are allotted for Up · Down traffic: UPPER HORWICH ST. } UP
CHORLEY STREET.

LOWER HORWICH ST. } DOWN
THORSEBY STREET.

1.

ORDERS FOR MOVEMENT
INTO ASSEMBLY POSITION

9ᵗʰ Bn York & Lancaster Regt

(1) DISTRIBUTION OF ATTACK IN ASSEMBLY POSITION

"A" Coy in LIVERPOOL STREET.
"B" Coy BAMBERBRIDGE STREET. & new but into front line Trenches.
"C" Coy QUARRYBRAE STREET. (nearest front trenches)
"D" Coy QUARRYBRAE. ST (GLASGOW ST end)
Bn HQs QUARRY POST.

(2) At a time to be stated later the Bn will move into position of Assembly as above.
The movement will be carried out by Platoons at 5 minutes interval in the following order, via communication trenches as below mentioned:-

"B" Coy
Moving via UPPER HORWICH ST - QUARRY POST - CHORLEY STREET to BAMBERBRIDGE. STREET.

8.

"C" Coy   via UPPER HORWICH ST —
          QUARRYBRAE ST.

"D" Coy   As per "C" Coy

"A" Coy   UPPER HORWICH. ST — QUARRY POST.
          — CHORLEY ST. — CHORLEY STEPS. —
          LIVERPOOL ST.

(3)
DRESS.   Fighting Order — Waterproof sheets
          will be carried.

(4)
REGTL.   1st Line Transport consisting of S.A.A.
TRANSPORT.   carts, NIL — 8 pack animals for S.A.A.
          — 2 water carts — 4 field kitchens —
          1 Officers Mess cart — 1 Medical
          cart — 2 tool wagons — 2 Lewis Gun lim-
          bers — will be parked in LONG VALLEY
          under Lt. PAINE. Bde T.O.
          2nd Line Transport — remainder
          to be in HENNENCOURT WOOD under
          Senior T.O. present.

(5)
STORES   According to instructions &
DUMPS   maps issued.
─────
BN
ADVANCED Are established at the
STORES   following points:-

9

1. Junction of LONGRIDGE ST & front line.
2. ½ way between LONGRIDGE ST & QUARRYBRAE ST.
3. Trench end of QUARRYBRAE ST.
4. Junction of BAMBERBRIDGE ST & front line.
5. Front line between BAMBERBRIDGE ST & STANLEY ST.
6. Trench ~~end of Stanley~~ STANLEY STREET.

BRIGADE STORES   Brigade Stores are at QUARRY POST STANLEY ST

RATION DUMP   GLASGOW ROAD
" WATER   COOKHOUSE, QUARRY POST.

(6)
BN AID POST & DRESSING STATION   Advanced Dressing Station is situated near QUARRY POST.

(7)
REPORTS.   OC Coys will report to Bn HQs as soon as their Coys are in position.

10

ATTACK ORDERS.

1.
ATTACK FORMATION.

At Zero minus 3 minutes Light Trench Mortars will barrage front German line from point X.2.c.1.1 as far as point X.2.a.2.4.

At Zero the two front waves of the assaulting Bns will advance to the attack & their 3rd & 4th waves commence to move out in succession into "NO MAN'S LAND." At the same moment the 9 Y & L Regt will commence to move into our front line trenches into the position of readiness. Coys taking up the following positions:-

<u>C Coy</u> With its right resting on LONGRIDGE ST. left on QUARRYBRAE ST (inclusive)

<u>D Coy.</u> From QUARRYBRAE ST (exclusive) to sap No 2 in X.4. (inclusive).

<u>B Coy.</u> From Sap NO 2 in X.1.1. (exclusive) to the HORN. (inclusive)

11

A Coy From the HORN (exclusive) to Sap N0 4 (inclusive) This Coy moving via STANLEY. ST.

2
THE ADVANCE — As soon as the 4th Wave of the assaulting Bns evacuates the German front line trench the 1st Wave of the 9 Y&L will cross our parapets move forward to the German front line trench — The 2nd Wave 9 Y&L will remain in our own front line trench until their first wave has evacuated the German front line trench when they will also move forward to occupy that trench & the attack will be carried out in successive waves in this manner. The 9 Y&L will attack as per sketch with 2 platoons per Coy in each wave.

A. Coy	B. Coy	D. Coy	C. Coy
2 Plns	2 Plns	2 Plns	2 Plns
2 Plns	2 Plns	2 Plns	2 Plns

12

(3) FRONTAGE & ZONE OF ATTACK

The frontage of the Bn. will be equal to the whole Brigade frontage the Right flank of 'C' Coy.
will move by the following points:-
2/11 - 2/85 - 2/28 - 2/62 - 2/90 - 2/94
3/40 - 3/30 - 33/85 - 33/95 - 34/27
34/48 - 34/91.

The left flank of "A" Coy
will move by points:-
2/22 - 2/43 - 2/56 - 32/12 - 32/23 -
32/67 to a point about 50 yards
N of 32/55 - to a point about 100
yards N of 34/28.

(4) ARTILLERY BARRAGE

During the attack the artillery barrage will "lift" at the following moments:-
(1) From "1st point to be consoledated" at 0.30 minutes.
(2) From "2nd position to be consoledated" at 1.25.

(5) COMMUNICATION

The OC 'C' Coy will be responsible for keeping touch with 25th Bde on our right.

13

The OC A Coy will be responsible for getting into touch with the 32nd Division on our left flank at the earliest opportunity.

(6) LIAISON

Lt Else & 4 men already detailed will act as LIAISON Officer & party between the 8th KOYLI & the 9th Y&L.

2/Lt GEAKE & 4 men already detailed will act in a like capacity between the 8th Y&L & 9th Y&L.

These Officers will report themselves to the HQrs of the respective Bns at one hour before the zero hour.

Their duties are to keep the OC 9 Y&L informed as to progress made by the assaulting Bns throughout the action.

Communication between waves will also be maintained by the use of boy battle-scouts.

(7) CLEARING-UP & BOMBING PARTIES

Coy Commanders will detail bombing parties to "clear-up" each successive line of trenches occupied, & the communication trenches between each line etc.

14.

Though these trenches have been crossed by the assaulting Bns. there may be a considerable number of the enemy still left in the dug-outs who must be dealt with.

(8) PRISONERS GUARD. Coy Commanders will detail special parties to act as guards to prisoners & conduct them back to "D" Bn. Sherwood Foresters) Strength at the rate of 1 man per 15 prisoners. These prisoners guards should carry bombs. After handing over the prisoners they will rejoin their Coys.

(9) LEWIS GUNS One Lewis gun will move with each Coy front line & one Lewis gun will each accompany the second line.
The four latter will be under the orders of the Commanding Officer. The men of the detachments must be actually in the ranks of Platoons.

Every N.C.O. & men in the Bn. 15
will carry two Mells Bombs
each. Extra Bombs will be
carried by Bombing Parties according to instructions issued.

(11)
S.A.A.   Each N.C.O & Man except Bombers
& Machine Gunners will in add-
ition to their 120 rounds already carried, carry two extra bandoliers, making
in all 220 rounds per man.
Bombers will carry 120 rounds
only. Machine Gunners 50 rounds
only.
10 boxes per Coy as Lewis Gun S.A.A.
will also be carried forward
by Coys. These boxes will be
dumped in the German front
line trenches at the following
points:-
"C" Coy dump near point 24
"D"   "   "   "   "   37
"B"   "   "   "   "   39
"A"   "   "   "   "   22

16.

(12) SANDBAGS — Every N.C.O. & man will carry four sandbags. These will be carried at the back, passed through between the back & the equipment braces.

(13) TOOLS — Each Coy will carry about 16 picks & 32 shovels — these will be slung on the mans back with a cord which will be issued.
These tools will be carried by men in the second line.

(14) WATER — All water bottles will be filled by _____ of Y/Z night. This water must not be drunk while the Bn is still in our own trenches & is only to be used when absolutely necessary — as it may be many hours before water bottles can be replenished. This must be specially impressed on the men.

(15) IRON RATIONS — Iron Rations & the unconsumed portions of the days rations will be carried in Haversack.

17

(16) BN ADVANCED DUMPS. A Bn Advanced ration dump will be formed in the German front line as far forward as possible when circumstances permit.

(17) SIGNALLERS Will act according to arrangements made by the Signalling Officer. A copy of scheme has been sent to Coy Commanders.

(18) REGTL AID POST. The M.O will select - after the advance - a suitable position for Regtl Aid Post & will at once inform Coy Commanders & Bn H.Qrs as to its position.

(19) Cancelled

(20) STEPS & LADDERS. When hostile trenches have been occupied steps must be cut in the wall of the parados (when no ladders are available) to enable men to get quickly out of the trench.

18

(21) CHARGE OF S.A.A.
The Regtl Sgt-Major assisted by the pioneers will have charge of the Coy & Lewis Gun ammunition in the advanced Dump (1st German Trench) & will superintend the forwarding of the boxes of S.A.A. to Coys as required.

(22) SNIPERS
Coy Commanders will instruct their snipers to be exceptionally busy during the artillery bombardment.

(23) REPAIRS TO PARAPET IN OUR TRENCHES
During bombardment Coys will be responsible for repairs to trenches, &c which may become necessary.

(24) RIFLE FIRE
Rifle fire will be used during the period of the smoke barrage.

(25) RANGE CARDS.
Range Cards will be provided to all Lewis Guns, showing targets, during bombardment & the advance.

		19
(26) SYSTEM OF HOSTILE BAR-RAGE.	During our gas & smoke attack all Officers will carefully note the system of barrages established by the enemy.	
(27) STRETCHER BEARERS.	The Bn Stretcher Bearers belong essentially to their own Bns & if heavy casualties occur should keep as far forward as possible, rendering first aid. The R.A.M.C. should clear bad casualties & stretcher cases. To enable this to be done Bn Stretcher Bearers should each be given a written order (to be shown if necessary) stating that they have orders to rejoin their units at once & are not to take orders from anyone except their own Medical Officers or one of their own Bn Officers.	
(28) MISCELLANEOUS	(a) No papers or orders are to be carried by Officers, NCOs or men taking part in the attack, except the new 1/5000 German trench.	

map - the 1/20000 map sheet 20.
57.D.S.E.
All messages or reports will refer to one or other of these maps.
(b) Hand grenades are not to be thrown indiscriminately as they are hard to replenish.
(c) Any guns captured, which are in danger of being lost, must be rendered useless by damaging sights & breach mechanism. Methods for doing this with pick axes, Mills Bombs or other expedients must be explained by Coy Commanders to all ranks. Machine Guns when captured must be collected & destroyed.

(29) SMOKE HELMETS.
On the night of the 17/18° & 18/19° inst - <u>all</u> officers, NCO's & men will wear their smoke helmets rolled on their heads.
These helmets should be exchanged with Ordnance for fresh ones on first convenient opportunity.

(30) Bn Hd. Qrs.
Bn Headquarters will move with our second wave & will be established at the following points

21.

2/39 - 2/81 - 2/03 - 2/48 - 2/78
33/41 - 33/74 - 33/26 - 33/78.

J Baldwin Lt Col
Comdg 79th N.Y. R+
Lancaster Ry

Issued 18-6-16

Copies 1   File
   "   2 & 3   A Coy
   "   4 & 5   B "
   "   6 & 7   C "
   "   8 & 9   D "
   "   10   2nd in Comd.
   "   11   Adjutant
   "   12   M.O.
   "   13   M.G.O
   "   14   Sig: Officer
   "   15   Bombing Officer
   "   16   Major Armstrong
   "   17   Q.M.
   "   18   T.O.

Instructions & orders for the Attack R

(1) Point of attack — The Battalion is detailed to attack the enemy's trenches between N.10.C.6.4 & N.10.D.1½.7½. Two companies will assault and two companies will be in support in our own trenches.

(2) Object — To kill as many of the enemy as possible, damage their trenches and mine shafts & take prisoners.

(3) Duration of operations — The time occupied in these operations to be 1 hour, counting from the hour the actual assault commences to the time of return to our own trenches.

(4) Hour of assault — Will be 2 hours before dawn. (N.B. dawn is 6.30 a.m.)

(5) Artillery Support — The R.F.A. Bde have done their utmost to cut enemy wire, but as all the wire cannot be seen, it cannot be taken for granted that the whole of the wire has been cut.

(6) Frontage of attack — The frontage of enemy line to be attacked is about 300 yards — extending from N.10.C.6.4 to N.10.D.1½.7½.

(7) Distribution of Companies — "A" & "C" Companies are detailed to carry out the attack.

"B" & "D" Companies to hold our own line of trenches, in support.

Before operation commences B. Coy will occupy the fire trenches from N.,3.C.5½.6 to the road leading to FERME DELAHTRE (inclusive) D Coy from this road (exclusive) to point N.10.a.9½.½

C. Coy will be in Assembly Trenches close in rear of "B" Coy

A. Coy those in rear of D. Coy with the latter occupying the same frontage as B & D Companies respectively.

(8) Advance to position of Readiness

The Advance to positions of Readiness will be commenced at 2 p.m. Platoons being led out by their Commanders through the Sally-ports – & will first line the borrow-trench in front of our parapet
The Advance from that point will be carried out as follows Platoons will be advanced to the next ditch running across our front, by driblets & placed in position by platoon Commanders – and so on till they reach the ditch nearest the Enemy lines, which has previously been held by a small covering party to prevent the enemy's occupation of the ditch –
The Assaulting Companies will form their companies as follows
Each Coy Comdr will

detail 2 platoons for the first
line & 2 platoons for the
second line.

(9) Objective — The objective of the 1st line of
platoons will be the
Enemy's Support trenches between
points
N.10.C.6.2 and
N.10.D.8.7.

Will these be time for this? RS

The objective of the 2nd line of
platoons will be the enemy's
front line trenches between
points previously stated

The first line of platoons
will advance without
pause to their objective

Both lines of platoons
will do as much
damage as they can

to the hostile trenches, kill
as many Germans as possible
and take prisoners.

(10) Time of Assault
The Assaulting Companies will
advance to the attack at
4.30 am at which hour
the Artillery will open
rapid fire at the enemy's
third line trenches,
communication trenches &
targets supposed to hold
troops.
The Vickers guns will
also support the attack by
overhead fire on the
hostile Comⁿ trenches &c.
as already arranged.
Fire from both will be
maintained on the hostile
trenches on each flank
of our attack.
The front platoons of the
Assaulting Companies will
carry all the wire-cutters available

(11)
Prisoners — so that each man shall have a pair.

All prisoners will be sent under escort to 2 points
N. 10. c. 7. 5 and
N. 10. c. 9½. 6½
by the respective companies & handed over to guards there which will be furnished by the O.C. B. & D. Companies respectively.

The O.C. B & D Companies will each detail a guard of
1. Officer
1. Sergeant
1 Corporal
12 Privates
to the above mentioned points
This guard will conduct prisoners back to our own trenches & march them to Bn Advanced Headquarters —

(12)
Signallers. — The Signalling Officer will make arrangements for one signalling party to accompany each of the Assaulting Companies & to keep up communication with Bn Headquarters.

O.C. Cos would get the men from Signalling Officer but arrangements to be made by O.C. Cos H.Q.

(13)
Machine Guns — Six Lewis guns will be taken across to the enemy trenches in accordance with instructions already given.

(14)
Stretcher Bearers — Will accompany their Companies

(15)
Retirement. — The retirement of the

platoons holding the enemy's support trenches will be covered by bombers, machine guns, and the platoons holding the enemy's front line trenches. The retirement of the latter and the machine guns will be covered by Bombers.

The last of the Assaulting Companies should be in our own trenches by 5.30 a.m.

As the Assaulting Companies re-cross our own parapet they will proceed down to RUE PETILLON where they will be re-organized & marched back to the RUE du QUESNOY where billets have been prepared for them to rest in — & where a roll-call will be made.

(16) Supporting Companies — The Companies in support will continue to hold the line of our trenches until 9 a.m. when, if circumstances permit, they will be relieved by the 8th Bn. K.O.Y.L.I. They will then proceed to billets at RUE du QUESNOY.

(17) Reports — Reports as to progress, and situation will be made frequently to Bn. Ad'd Head Quarters.

Don't think this possible ←

Issued to All Officers

J Addison Lt Col
Comdg 9th Y & L Reg

I think platoon Cos. must have to arrange when to retire.
Special parties told off for maintaining connection between the 2 Cos.
Special men told off to damage parapet & dugouts
P.T.O.

1 Royal Irish Rifles
2nd Middlesex Regt
9th York & Lancaster Regt

W.P.131.
Secret

1. Gas cylinders are being placed in the front line from ARGYLE ST – THORSBY ST on the nights of 21/22nd and 22/23rd inst.

2. The following communication trenches, which are the routes being used by the carrying parties, must be left free from the hours named until the whole work is complete.

PRESTON AVENUE HODDER ST PALATINE ARGYLE RUSSIAN SAP DORSET ST PORT LOUIS	From 9.30pm on nights of 21/22 and 22/23.
JOHN OF GAUNT BARROW ST GOOSE DUBS RUSSIAN SAP RYECROFT PORT LOUIS	Ditto.

LANCASTER AVENUE ⎫ From 9.40 pm
RIVINGTON   ⎬ nights of 21/22 and 22/23.
~~ALDA~~ RYECROFT ⎪
PORT LOUIS   ⎭

LANCASTER AVENUE ⎫ From 10.40 pm
RIVINGTON   ⎬ night of 21/22
WALTNEY   ⎪ from 10 pm
LONGRIDGE   ⎪ night of 22/23.
PENDLE HILL   ⎪
WENNING ST   ⎭

✓ LOWER HORWICH ⎫ From 10 pm nights
✓ THORSBY   ⎬ of 21/22 and 22/23.
  WALTNEY   ⎪
✓ LONGRIDGE   ⎪
  PENDLE HILL   ⎪
  WENNING ST   ⎭

3. After the cylinders have been emplaced battalions in the trenches will assist the R.E. in replacing the sandbags over the emplacements.

.... Captain
20.6.16 /w Brigade Major 25th Inf. Bde.

70th Brigade
23rd Division.

1/9th BATTALION

YORKS & LANCS REGIMENT

AUGUST 1 9 1 6

Army Form C.2118.

Vol 9

1 Bn 3-9-1916

Q. Yolam

WAR DIARY
INTELLIGENCE SUMMARY
(Erase heading not required.)

Place	Date 1916 August	Hour	Summary of Events and Information	Remarks and references to Appendices
	1st		Battn. relieved by the 8th K.O.Y.L.I. about 6 P.M. and on relief took up position X.20. to X.26. near BECOURT WOOD.	
	2nd		attack practised in the morning.	
	3rd/4th		Bathing parade in the morning. Attack practised in the evenings. 2nd Lt. J.B. Montagu & 2nd Lt. J.B. Fawsitt joined Bn. (3rd inst)	
	5th		Physical drill in the early morning. During the whole of the night hostile artillery very active.	
	6th/7th		Orders received to move to FRANVILLERS on the 7th inst. Battn. left position near Becourt Wood at 7 A.M. and marched to FRANVILLERS — arrived there about 12 noon. — billets.	
	8th/9th		In billets at FRANVILLERS.	
	10th		Orders received for the Battn. to march to FRECHENCOURT, and entrain there on the 11th inst.	
	11th		Left FRANVILLERS 7-30 A.M. and marched to FRECHENCOURT STN where Battn. entrained. Detained at LONGRÉ STN at 8-30 P.M? and marched to PONT REMY arriving there about midnight — in billets.	

WAR DIARY
or
INTELLIGENCE SUMMARY

Army Form C. 2118.

Place	Date	Hour	Summary of Events and Information	Remarks and references to Appendices
	1916 August			
	12		In billets at PONT REMY	
	13		Batt. entrained at PONT REMY STN at 1-30 AM. Detrained at BAILLEUL STN at 12 noon, and marched to billets at METEREN.	
	14		Left METEREN 3.45 P.M. and marched to forward area (A.10.) arriving about 6 P.M. - billets	
	15		Left forward area at 3 AM and marched to billets in reserve area and relieved the 12th East Surrey Regt at 7 A.M. (Batt. in billets at SOYER FARM. DELENELLE. TILLEUL.)	
	16		In reserve area.	
	17		Relieved 10th Queen's Regt. in the trenches at 7 AM. Two Coys. in the front line, one in support, and one in reserve. Hostile Artillery very quiet. 50 men worked on close support line, parapets improved & made bullet proof.	
	18		More wire put out in weak places in our wire defences, new site prepared for Coy. H.Qrs. Main communication trenches improved. Our Snipers active. Enemy fired a few shells in BURNT OUT FARM. LANCASHIRE SUPPORT FM. & AYR STREET from 2 P.M. to 3 P.M. Wire defences improved. 2nd Lt. J. V. Medley & 2nd Lt. Blee joined Batt.	
	19			
	20			

WAR DIARY
or
INTELLIGENCE SUMMARY
(Erase heading not required.)

Army Form C. 2118

Place	Date 1916 August	Hour	Summary of Events and Information	Remarks and references to Appendices
	21st		Our Snipers active during the day. Hostile M.G.'s active all night. Further improvements made on GLOUCESTER FORT. Hon. enlargements obtained. 2nd Lt. P.L. Gordon slightly wounded in the head. Capt. Buxton R.A.M.C. joined Batt. vice Lt. Mackay R.A.M.C. sick to F.A.	
	22nd		Indirect searching fire by the enemy on LANCASHIRE SUPPORT FARM & the enemy line from "MAISON 73".	
	23rd		At about 10-30 A.M. enemy shelled T109 & communication trench with 77mm. Orders received that the Batt. would be relieved by the 10th Northumberland Fusiliers at 6 A.M. on the 24th.	
	24th		On being relieved by the 10th N.F.'s the Batt. marched to billets at & about PONT DE NIEPPE. Sic transit drill etc.	
	25th		Continuation of training whilst in billets.	
	26th		Recd. visit Lt. J. Price (Wellington) & other men who had gained honours. Maj. Gen. J.W. Bubbington C.B. C.M.G. Batt. in Working parties. D/Lt. (Hon) G. Colonel Ken by F.G.C.M.	
	27th		Working parties provided.	
	28th			
	29th		Continued training, lectures etc. (Divisional Baths allotted to the Batt.)	

Army Form C. 2118

WAR DIARY
or
INTELLIGENCE SUMMARY

(Erase heading not required.)

Instructions regarding War Diaries and Intelligence Summaries are contained in F. S. Regs., Part II. and the Staff Manual respectively. Title Pages will be prepared in manuscript.

Place	Date	Hour	Summary of Events and Information	Remarks and references to Appendices
	1916 August 30		Continued with training & Lectures on Anti - Gas appliances etc. 2nd Lt R. Kerry joined the Battalion.	
	31st		Short route march in the morning, Gas Helmet drill etc in the afternoon.	

A.F. Palmer Lt. Col.
Comdg. 9th Bn. York & Lancaster Regt.

Honours List.

2nd Lt. H. Bagley — D.S.O.
Sergt. T. V. Prior — M.C.
No. 18635 Pte. Elliott H.H. — D.C.M.
15482 " Reeves
17.0367 " Bullen
15.4763 " Bramwell
12.7086 " Jones G.
19.066 " Marshall
14.866 " Woodcock
19.563 " Willworth, E.

16.888 Sjt. Brannon S.
15.394 " Mellor S.
192/23 L/Sjt. Clifford S.
                  L/Sjt. Baxter, V.H.J.

⎫
⎬ Military Medal.
⎭

Casualties for month ending August 31st 1916

1. Officer wounded
1. O.R. killed
7. O.R's wounded

Army Form C. 2118.

WAR DIARY
or
INTELLIGENCE SUMMARY
(Erase heading not required.)

Vol 10

20/23

9th York & Lancs.

Place	Date	Hour	Summary of Events and Information	Remarks and references to Appendices
	1916 Sept 1st		Battn. at PONT-DE-NIEPPE. Orders were received that the Battn. would take over trenches on the 2nd inst. Later these orders were cancelled and we moved to METEREN AREA on the 2nd.	
	2nd		Left PONT-DE-NIEPPE at 1-30 P.M. and marched to billets in METEREN AREA arriving about 5 P.M. Orders received to move to WALLON-CAPPEL on the 3rd.	
	3rd		Paraded 9 A.M. and marched to WALLON-CAPPEL arrived billets about 2 P.M. Orders received that Battn. would move to billets in ARQUES on the 4th.	
	4th		Arrived ARQUES about 1 P.M. and received orders to move on the 6th to LUMBRES.	
	5th		Marched to LUMBRES & arrived about 2 P.M.	
	6th		In billets at LUMBRES. Special training was carried out.	
	7th		Training continued. Parties detailed in readiness for billeting & looking of train.	
	8th		Advanced billeting party left St Omer Station at 2 A.M. for AMIENS AREA. Loyd's Battimid training.	
	9th		Major General Ed. Babbington C.B.J.C.M.G. inspected the Battn. (B Coy at full marching order) Orders received that Battn. would move.	

2449 Wt. W14957/M90 750,000 1/16 J.B.C. & A. Forms/C.2118/12.

WAR DIARY or INTELLIGENCE SUMMARY

Army Form C. 2118.

Place	Date	Hour	Summary of Events and Information	Remarks and references to Appendices
	1916 Sept 10th		The Battn. left LUMBRES at 9 A.M. and marched to ST. OMER STN. and entrained at 12-45 P.M. Detrained at LONGUEAU STN. and marched to billets in CARDONETTE arriving about 2 A.M. on the 11th inst. 2nd Lt. W.M. McCubbin joined the Battn. 2 H.L.C. Blue & Hoo.	
	12th		Battn. left Becourt Wood in buses & arrived in camp near BECOURT WOOD at 12-30 P.M. Battn. now under orders of 46th Inf. Bde. Two working parties supplied, one for the 2nd Gordons (2 officers & 200 O.R's) and 11 officers & 400 other ranks, working under orders of the 46th Inf. Bde. 2nd Lt. Lawson-Brown - wounded. Other ranks 2 killed, 4 wounded.	
	13th		Working parties again supplied for the trenches. Casualties - 2nd Lt. R.L. Gordon wounded - other ranks 5 killed, 15 wounded.	
	14th		Battn. left camp about 7-30 P.M. & took up position in BOURAY TRENCH, in reserve to 45th Inf. Bde. Casualties 2 other ranks wounded.	
	15th		Two Battns. of the 46th Inf. Bde. attacked the German lines & took final objective. 7 offrs. & 265 O.R's being taken prisoner. About 8 P.M. the Battn. less B Coy relieved the 10th Sco. Ruf. & 7/8 K.O.S.B. in front line (PUSH ALLEY) B Coy coming under orders of the 12 H.L.I. Battn. HdQrs. remained at BOURAY TRENCH	

WAR DIARY
or
INTELLIGENCE SUMMARY

(Erase heading not required.)

Army Form C. 2118.

Place	Date Sept.	Hour	Summary of Events and Information	Remarks and references to Appendices
	15th		Batt. advanced Hd. Qrs. was established close behind the front line. 2nd Lt. W.N. McKibbing to hos. sick. — Casualties 1 O.R. killed 2 O.R. wounded.	
	16th		The Batt. established two strong advanced posts in front of PUSH ALLEY. About 9 P.M. the Batt. was relieved by the 10/11th H.L.I. and marched to bivouac in BLACK WOOD, and rejoined 7th Bde. Casualties 2nd Lt. Y.B. Favritt killed. other ranks. 6 killed, 30 wounded.	
	17th 18th		Orders received to move to SHELTER WOOD on the 18th. Batt. marched to SHELTER WOOD AREA at 7-30 A.M. and relieved the 7/8th K.O.S.B. — Casualties 3 other ranks wounded.	
	19th 20th 21st		Batt. in SHELTER WOOD AREA, on the 21st one man accidently injured.	
	22nd		In the evening the Batt. was relieved by the 10th WEST RIDING REGT. and Companies took up new dispositions immediately in front of Batt. Hd Qrs. — B.M. 2nd Lt. H. Hamilton R.A.M.C. joined the Batt. vice, Lt. R.A. Marler sick.	
	23rd		Batt. billeted at "A" dump BECOURT WOOD. Lt-Col A.T.B. ADDISON'S body found in "NO MAN'S LAND" near AVELEY WOOD & OVILLERS	

WAR DIARY
or
INTELLIGENCE SUMMARY

(Erase heading not required.)

Army Form C. 2118.

Place	Date Sept	Hour	Summary of Events and Information	Remarks and references to Appendices
	24th		Battn in camp near SHELTER WOOD. Lieut C.F.B. Hensley joined the Battn. and took over command "A" Company the funeral of the late Lt Col A.J.B. Addison took place at the Cemetery	
	25th		BECOURT WOOD at 3-0. P.M. Battn. relieved the 11th Northumberland Fusiliers in support line Bn. H.A. Qrs in O.G.1. Companies occupied trench in front of O.G.1. A working party of 2 officers & 100 O.R. was supplied for the forward trenches	
	26th		Situation normal. Work was carried out, improving, repairing & building dug outs etc. In the evening 2 officers & 100 O.R. were detailed to work under the R.E. 10 Battery on the front line	
	27th		Situation normal. Work on trench continued a party of 2 3.O.R. with an officer assisted in laying cable as far forward as possible. The Battn. relieved the 2nd KOYLI in the front line trenches. Bn. H.A. Qrs MARTIN PUICH.	
	28th		Battn. worked in improving the consolidation of the trench, late 8 officers & 400 O.R. worked under the orders and supervision of the R.E. 10 O.R. (slight) were also wounded	
	29th			

Army Form C. 2118.

WAR DIARY
or
INTELLIGENCE SUMMARY

(Erase heading not required.)

Instructions regarding War Diaries and Intelligence Summaries are contained in F.S. Regs., Part II. and the Staff Manual respectively. Title Pages will be prepared in manuscript.

Place	Date	Hour	Summary of Events and Information	Remarks and references to Appendices
	30.6		Work on trench continued. Batt. moved into assembly positions as follows:- A Coy M26 b 5.3 to M26 b 1.1. B Coy M26 b 1.1 to M26 a 7.0. C Coy M26 a 7.0 to M26 c 2.9. D Coy M26 c 2.9 to M26 c 5.3. In the evening working party commenced work on a new trench from a point about M26 b 7.6. Casualties for the month Killed:- 2nd Lt. J.B. Hewitt. 14 other ranks. WOUNDED:- 2nd Lt. Lauron-Brown. 2nd Lt. O.L. Gordon. 85 other ranks. SHELL SHOCK:- 14 other ranks.	

A.A.Murray Lt.Col
Commdg. 9th Bn. York & Lancs

Army Form C. 2118.

WAR DIARY
or
INTELLIGENCE SUMMARY
(Erase heading not required.)

70/23 October 1916 9th York & Lancs Vol III

Place	Date	Hour	Summary of Events and Information	Remarks and references to Appendices
	Oct 1/10		Battalion in assembly positions in 26 Avenue. About 3 P.M. Three Companies moved forward to JUMPING OFF TRENCH. Supports were sent to the K.O.Y.L.I. on the left of the BAPAUME RD who were in a critical position. Several patrols were sent out to gain information regarding the left flank and to get in touch with the K.O.Y.L.I. but reported that they could not get in touch with them at all. Casualties – Capt Power, Francis Evans, Lt Leahy wounded – Lt Hendly wounded. O.R. 4 killed, 10 wounded	
	Oct 2		About 3 a.m. a report was received from Capt McCrea stating their reinforcements were urgently needed. Two remaining Coys and two Vickers Guns which had been attached for Anty Duties the day were sent up by order of the C.O. – These Coys for into position about 4–30 A.M. between the K.O.Y.L.I. and the 6th Corps of W. Yorks in O.G.1. – Blocks were immediately made in the Communication Trench. About 9 P.M. the enemy made a bombing attack on O.G.1 which were repulsed. Casualties: O.R. 21 Killed; 61 Wounded; 28 Missing	
	Oct 3		The Battn was relieved by the West Riding Regt about 6 A.M. and took up position at the "Dingle" – orders were received stating that Bn would move to Franvillers and Clarke Trench on the 4th inst. Casualties O.R. 7 Killed; 16 Wounded; 3 Missing.	

Army Form C. 2118.

WAR DIARY
or
INTELLIGENCE SUMMARY

(Erase heading not required.)

Instructions regarding War Diaries and Intelligence Summaries are contained in F.S. Regs., Part II. and the Staff Manual respectively. Title Pages will be prepared in manuscript.

Place	Date	Hour	Summary of Events and Information	Remarks and references to Appendices
	4/10/16		No 19173 Pte H Taylor awarded Military Medal by the C in C. Compensatory. 2nd R.? Keatly to England. During the morning the Dispositions were made into SWANSEA TRENCH and CLARKS TRENCH were cancelled. The Battn at the Dingle	
	5.10.16		" " " "	
	6.10.16		" " " "	
	7.10.16		The Battn left the DINGLE about 9-30 A.M. and marched to SWANSEA TRENCH and CLARKS TRENCH arriving there about 11-30 AM. Casualties – Nil	
	8.10.16		Orders received in the early morning that the Battn would remain at X29 Central. Afternoon at VIVIER MILL when march to BRESLE, that orders were cancelled later and the Bn. By their Dispositions about 5-30 P.M. and marched to BECOURT WOOD. Arriving there about 9 P.M. when they bivouaced for the night. Casualties: - 2 O.R. Wounded.	
	9/10/16		The Battn left BECOURT WOOD at 10 A.M. and marched to Camp at BRESLE Arriving there at about 12-30 P.M.	
	10.10.16		On at BRESLE. The day was devoted to Interior economy. 2nd Lt F DAVIES joined the Battn. Orders were received regarding the moving of the Transport on the 11th inst.	
	11.10.16		The Transport moved by road to the New Area — At 3 A.M. The C in C Common-wealth inspected the Brigade.	

Army Form C. 2118.

WAR DIARY
or
INTELLIGENCE SUMMARY
(Erase heading not required.)

Place	Date	Hour	Summary of Events and Information	Remarks and references to Appendices
	12-10-16		The Battn left BRESLE at 11 A.M. and marched to ALBERT where they entrained at 5-30 P.M.	
	13-10-16		The Battn detrained at LONG PRE Station about 9-30 A.M. and marched to BICELES via PONT REMY. Arriving here at 12 Noon. A Coy reported at ST RIQUIER Station at 4 P.M. and assisted the remainder of the Division in entraining etc. Capt. E.V. PRICE granted extension of leave by Medical Board on account of sickness. The Battn left PONT REMY at 6.45 A.M. and marched to NEUF MOULIN arriving here in Billets at 12 Noon.	
	14-10-16			
	15-10-16		Battn in Billets at NEUF MOULIN, the transport moved about 10 P.M. to ST RIQUIER Station. "B" Coy also moved with the transport and assisted in loading.	
	16-10-16		The Battn left NEUF MOULIN at 1-30 A.M. and marched to ST RIQUIER Arriving they entrained at 3 A.M. – Detrained at 11 A.M. at PROVEN and marched to Camp at Q 23 a 9.7 (Scottish LINES) Arriving about 4 P.M.	
	17-10-16		Battn entrained on Railway Siding (G.S.C.) at 5-30 P.M. Arriving at YPRES SIDINGS (I 7 C.4.3.) and took up position in ZILLEBEKE BUND at 9 P.M. 2nd Lt P.E. SHARPLES granted leave. 2nd Lt A.G. PRICE (A/Adj) to Hospital (sick) Capt J.T. POWER granted extension of leave (Auth CR No 1536/1051/R. Casualties – nil.	
	18-10-16		Battn relieved the 7th Australian Bn in the Front line at 10 P.M. M.H. SWARBS at VALLEY COTTAGES – Three Companies in Front line one in Support Casualties – nil.	

WAR DIARY
or
INTELLIGENCE SUMMARY

(Erase heading not required.)

Army Form C. 2118.

Instructions regarding War Diaries and Intelligence Summaries are contained in F. S. Regs., Part II and the Staff Manual respectively. Title Pages will be prepared in manuscript.

Place	Date	Hour	Summary of Events and Information	Remarks and references to Appendices
	19.10.16		Batt. in Dispositions as on 18th — 4 officers temporarily attached Infantry Carracts — 1 O.R. Killed 1 O.R. Wounded	
	20.10.16		Batt. in Dispositions as on the 18th — Casualties — Nil 4 Officers temporarily attached to Batt — Lt. R.S. LYNDEN — 2nd LT A. BARBER 2 LT. C.S. TOMLINSON - 2nd LT A.D. SWALE = Cmlty 70th Bde No 792 of 20.10.16. Batt. relieved by the 11th SHERWOOD FORESTERS at 9 P.M. and took up positions in ZILLEBEKE BUND — Relief completed at 11 P.M.	
	22.10.16		Batt. at ZILLEBEKE BUND Working parties supplied consisting of 3 officers and 145 O.R.	
	23.10.16		Batt. at "BUND" — Working party supplied consisting of 1 Officer and 50.O.R. The Box RESPIRATORS of the Batt. were fitted and tested by GAS OFFICER. A number of men Bathed.	
	24.10.16		Batt. at THE BUND. A number of men Bathed — Lt. G.F.B. HANDLEY and 2 LT G. RIGBY awarded Military Cross — No 8992 C/Q.S.M. DOBSON J.P. awarded D.C.M. D.R.O. No 1925 of 24.10.16 Working parties were supplied consisting of 4 officers and 170 O.R.	
	25.10.16		Batt. at the BUND — Working parties supplied consisting of 3 Officers and 200. O.R. Orders received with regard to the Batts. Relieving the 11th Cheshire Touches in the line on the 26th.	
	26.10.16		The Brigadier General decorated 2nd LT G. RIGBY (Military Cross) and C/R.S.M. DOBSON J.P. (D.C.M) at Brigade H. Quarters — On relieve the 11th Cheshire Pioneers in Front Line — Relief completed in the Front Line, one Coy in Support — Relief complete at 10 P.M. Bn H. Quarters at VALLEY COTTAGES	

Army Form C. 2118.

WAR DIARY
or
INTELLIGENCE SUMMARY
(Erase heading not required.)

Instructions regarding War Diaries and Intelligence Summaries are contained in F.S. Regs., Part II. and the Staff Manual respectively. Title Pages will be prepared in manuscript.

Place	Date	Hour	Summary of Events and Information	Remarks and references to Appendices
	27.10.16 28.10.16		Coys in Dispositions as on 26th. Enemy opened fire on our front line trenches with his trench mortars - our trench mortars retaliating - Casualties - 1 O.R. wounded. Operation orders received in the evening respecting Relief.	
	29.10.16		Coys in above Dispositions Casualties - 2 O.R. killed The 10th Northum. Fusiliers relieved the 9th Y. & L. in the evening - Relief complete about 11.20 P.M.	
	30.10.16		The Batt. after Relief entrained at YPRES STATION sidings for POPERINGHE. Arrived in Billets about 3 A.M. 2nd Lt. Sharp too returned from leave Pte. L.S. Riddell to Hospital, sick.	
	31.10.16		Batt. in Billets at POPERINGHE - At 11 A.M. The Brigade were inspected by the Army Commander. The Batt. bathed in the afternoon. Major D. Quirk joined the Batt.	

1.11.16

D. Quirk Major
Cmdg. 9th York & Lancaster Regt.

ORDERLY ROOM
2 NOV 1916
9th BN. YORK & LANC. REGT.

WAR DIARY or INTELLIGENCE SUMMARY

Army Form C. 2118.

9th York & Lancs Vol 12

Place	Date	Hour	Summary of Events and Information	Remarks and references to Appendices
	1916. Nov 1st		The Battn in billets at Popering̃he – 2nd Turton proceeded on leave – 2 2nd Bannatt joined the Battalion – 2nd Morley and one NCO & 6 men proceeded to Toners Camp Rest School for Lewis Gun Course	
	Nov 2nd		Major D. Quirk 8th Batt. for "Lancaster Regt" took over temporary command of K9 for Lancaster Regt – Lt. Col Palmer proceeded on leave – Capt S.V. Price received a further extension of leave for 14 days on 25 Oct 1916 a medical board (Auth. A.P.3.175) Batt. O.O. No. 113 received	
	Nov 3 Nov 4		Promulgation of F.G.C.M. of A/Cpl Warkington G.R. Pyne L'Cpl Ford Moore held under C.C. war au general supervision of O.C.M.A. No 16277 L/Cpl Corney W. and No 19940 Pte Cottrell E were evacuated by the R.O.C. Division at B.O. Ha Q.O. The Battn entrained at point Q.3.C.4.2 at 6.45 PM and relieved to 9th Batts. Yorkshire Regt. in Batt Reserve, in billets at the Barracks Ypres. Relief complete 7-30 PM.	
	Nov 5th		Batt in Batt Reserve in the Barracks Ypres. During the day the men were practised in Box respirator drill – Provisional Defence Scheme were issued in the event of the Batt having to move up to reinforce the Front Line in case of Serious Bombardment 2nd Lt. O.G. Price (Acting Adj.) evacuated to England Sick Auth. 2nd Army No. A/2157/49 dated 5/11/16 SRO No. 1996 dated 6/11/16 – Working parts supplies Consisting of 30 men and 20 O.R.	

Army Form C. 2118.

WAR DIARY
or
INTELLIGENCE SUMMARY

(Erase heading not required.)

Instructions regarding War Diaries and Intelligence Summaries are contained in F.S. Regs., Part II. and the Staff Manual respectively. Title Pages will be prepared in manuscript.

Place	Date	Hour	Summary of Events and Information	Remarks and references to Appendices
	1916 Nov 6		Baths in Mess Room at the Barracks Ypres — OC "B" & "D" Coys reconnoitred the front line taking particular note of the route to be taken by their Coys in case of the Battn. had to reinforce the firing line. Bn respirator drill practised — Lecture for all officers by Acting Officer. Capt L. NORRIS evacuated to England vide Ambce 2nd Army No 2457/50 dated 6/11/16	
	Nov 7		Working party of 2 Officers and 105 OR. Supplied — Casualties 3 OR. wounded. Baths in Mess Room at the Barracks Ypres — Bn respirator drill practised. OC A & B Coys reconnoitre the front line taking special note of route in case the Batn had to reinforce the front line. A number of men bathed in the afternoon. One NCO and 12 Men "D" Coy proceeded to Bde school Toronto Camp for course of wiring. Working party supplied.	
	Nov 8.		Baths at Barrack Ypres — Working party supplied consisting of 3 Officers and 140 OR. Fort Mange — Lecture by Lt Col WATSON. D.S.O. as the Battle of — Subject 23 Gm. No 6/197/311 dated 8/11/16 approved of — 2nd Lt Palmer wearing L. Badges of the rank of Captain pending necessary authority being received. Baths at the Barracks Ypres — Fort Mange — A number of men bathed in the afternoon — A working party supplied consisting of 3 Officers and 140 OR.	INTELLIGENCE
	Nov 9			Bn O.O. No 142 Received

2449 Wt. W14957/M90 750,000 1/16 J.B.C. & A. Forms/C.2118/12.

WAR DIARY or INTELLIGENCE SUMMARY

Army Form C. 2118.

(Erase heading not required.)

Place	Date	Hour	Summary of Events and Information	Remarks and references to Appendices
	1916 Nov 10		Batts in Barracks Ypres — Foot Mirage — The Battn relieved the 11th Reserve Frontier in the Line — Relief complete about 7-30pm. D Coy on Left in Front line — C Coy on the Right 3 Pl in Front line, 1 Pl in Lovers Walk A Coy 2 Pl in WELLINGTON St 1 Pl in FORT St 1 Pl MAPLE COPSE — B Coy RITZ St Batt Hd Qrs at The TUILLERIES.	
	Nov 11		Companies in above dispositions — 1 NCO from each Company to B de School TORONTO Camp for a course of Anti Aircraft Instruction. Situation Normal — Casualties Nil —	
	Nov 12		Coys in above dispositions — 2nd Lt R D TURTON returned from leave 2 Lt T D MONTAGU 1 NCO & 6 men returned from Lewis Gun Course The following NCOs & men proceeded to TORONTO Camp for courses LEWIS GUN COURSE — 2nd Lt R. KERRY 1 NCO & 6 men from C Coy SNIPING COURSE — 4 men from D Coy BOMBING COURSE — 1 NCO & 4 men from each Coy. Situation Normal — Casualties Nil —	
	Nov 13		Coys in above dispositions — Capt C PALMER proceeded on leave. Situation Normal — Casualties Nil In the Evening 5-30pm A Coy relieved C Coy in the Line B " " " D " " "	

Army Form C. 2118.

WAR DIARY
or
INTELLIGENCE SUMMARY

(Erase heading not required.)

Instructions regarding War Diaries and Intelligence Summaries are contained in F.S. Regs., Part II and the Staff Manual respectively. Title Pages will be prepared in manuscript.

Place	Date	Hour	Summary of Events and Information	Remarks and references to Appendices
	1916 Nov 14		Coys in New dispositions – 2nd Lt H. Wood joined the Battalion and was posted to D Coy. Situation Normal – Casualties nil.	
	Nov 15.		Coys in dispositions as on the 14th inst – Bde O.O. No 115 received Casualties nil – Situation Normal –	
	Nov 16.		Coys in dispositions as on the 14th inst Casualties 2 OR wounded – Situation Normal In the evening the 11th Northumberland Fusiliers relieved the 9th York Lancs Regt in the line – Relief complete about 10·50 pm. after being relieved the Batt marched to Ypres Ridge and entrained as 12 midnight for Manchester – The Batt arrived in Camp (St Lawrence) about 1·50 a.m. on the 17th inst.	
	Nov 17		5 Officers joined the Batt. 2nd Lt J.M. Pearman A Coy. 2nd Lt T.H. Hughes B Coy. 2nd Lt Newton C Coy. 2nd Lt E.J. Radford C Coy. 2nd Lt J.W. Cooke D Coy. Lt Col A.E. Palmer Transferred to the 6th York Lancaster Regt and Handed over the Strength of his Batt. 1 NCO 42 Men (D Coy) returned from Mining Course Bath as St Lawrence Camp – Capt M. Lewis transferred to Second Army to be Bde Major. R.712 Bde Order C.R. No 3305/1668.13. – 1 NCO 242 men from C Coy proceeded on a course of WIRING.	

Army Form C. 2118.

WAR DIARY
or
INTELLIGENCE SUMMARY
(Erase heading not required.)

Instructions regarding War Diaries and Intelligence Summaries are contained in F.S. Regs., Part II. and the Staff Manual respectively. Title Pages will be prepared in manuscript.

Place	Date	Hour	Summary of Events and Information	Remarks and references to Appendices
	Nov 18		Major R. Ratliffe Worcestershire Regt attached 6th Connaught Rangers joined the Battalion.	
	Nov 19		Major R. Ratliffe took over temporary command of the Battn, a number of NCO's & men were inoculated	
	Nov 20		A number of NCO's & men were inoculated - Pte O.O. 116 received 2nd Cl. Tomlinson and 2nd Lt A.D. Swale joined per our Unit. The 11th Sherwood Foresters. - 2nd Lt H. Wood proceeded on leave	
	Nov 21		A return was held on the Canada Field Winnipeg Camp in Physical Training & Bayonet fighting. All available Officers NCO's attended 2nd Lt. M. Peakman to hospital sick.	
	Nov 22		2nd Lt. J.B. Montagu & 2nd Lt L.F. Davies to hospital sick The Battn entrained for Ypres and then moved to front line and relieved the 9th Bn. Yorkshire Regt - Relief complete 9.45 P.M. 8 am in front line — B Coy on the right — C Coy in the centre — A Coy in support Battn HQ. at Valley Cottages — Casualties — 4 men D Coy rets from Brigade Bombers Course	
	Nov 23		Coy in close disposition - Casualties Nil - Relieves Personnel 2nd Lt. Dornant proceeded on a Lewis Gun Course 1 NCO +6 men proceeded on a " " 4 NCO's returned from Divnl Drill Instructors 1 NCO 46 men rets from Bombing Class.	

2449 Wt. W14957/M90 750,000 1/16 J.B.C. & A. Forms/C.2118/12.

Army Form C. 2118.

WAR DIARY
or
INTELLIGENCE SUMMARY

(Erase heading not required.)

Instructions regarding War Diaries and Intelligence Summaries are contained in F. S. Regs., Part II. and the Staff Manual respectively. Title Pages will be prepared in manuscript.

Place	Date	Hour	Summary of Events and Information	Remarks and references to Appendices
	1916 Nov 24		Corps in Dispositions as on 23rd inst – Casualties Nil – Situation Normal – 2nd Lt R. KERRY 1 NCO and 6 men returned from Lewis gun Course. Capt E.V. PRICE returned from Leave. MAJOR J.H. BOWES WILSON 1st Bath: West Riding Regt attached to this Batt'n. Our NCO & 16 men proceeded to Pres School for Monthly Course. 4 NCOs 16 men proceeded on a Course of Special Drill Instruction. 1 NCO 16 men returned from a Lewis gun Course	
	Nov 25		2nd Lt E.J. RADFORD proceeded on a training Course. Casualties "C" Coy in the evening – Relief Complete 9.30pm. Situation Normal – Casualties Nil –	
	Nov 26		Boys in New Dispositions – 2nd Lt J.W. COOKE proceeded on a course of Instruction at the Divisional School – Situation Normal – Casualties Nil –	
	Nov 27 Nov 28		Coys in Dispositions as on 26th inst – Casualties Nil – Situation Normal – Batt'n in Dispositions as on 26th inst – Situation Normal – Casualties 2 O.R. Wounded	
	Nov 29		11" Richard Regt relieved the Batt'n in the line – Relief complete 7.30pm – After Relief the Batt'n moved to ZILLEBEKE BUND – Casualties Normal.	
	Nov 30		Batt'n at ZILLEBEKE BUND. 2nd Lt J.M. PEAKMAN returned from Hospital. 2 NCOs 30 men supplied during the morning on Working Party. 7 NCOs 180 men supplied during the evening as Working Party	

R. Ratcliff Major
Comdg 9th (S) York & Lanc Regt.

Army Form C. 2118.

York 5
9th YORK & LANCS

WAR DIARY
or
INTELLIGENCE SUMMARY.
(Erase heading not required.)

Instructions regarding War Diaries and Intelligence
Summaries are contained in F. S. Regs., Part II.
and the Staff Manual respectively. Title pages
will be prepared in manuscript.

Place	Date	Hour	Summary of Events and Information	Remarks and references to Appendices
	1916			
	Dec 1		The Battn in Lillers Burd - A working party in the morning consisting of 3 NCOs & 60 men, and another in the Evening consisting of 8 NCOs and 180 men. Casualties 1 OR Accidentally wounded	
	2nd		The Battn in the BEUNE BUND working parties suppied as in prins - 2nd Lt Atrul returned from Leave. 2nd Lt Radford returned from Hygin; Course	
	3rd		The Battn in the Bund working parties suppied as on 1st inst - 2nd Lt Higson proceeded on Lewis gun Course - Major J T Bell Quartermaster proceeded on leave.	
	4th		The Battn in the Bund - Operation order 118 issued from Brigade - Working part suppied in the evening consisting of 10 officers 8 NCOs & 185 men - The premier signal was inspected by the G.O.C at Rue des Bois.	
	5th		The Battalion in the Bund - Dr R. Hamilton Medical Officer returned from leave Capt A Farqwar RAMC proceeded on leave - 2nd Lt C. Barnett N.Z.a from Lewis gun Course - The Battn relieved the 11th Sherwood Foresters in the line. Relief complete 9-30 p.m. Dispositions B Coy on the Right in front line, B Coy on Right in Front line, A Coy in the Centre, C Coy in Support Battn Hd Qr RUDKIN HALL - O.O. No 13 received - Casualties Nil Situation Normal -	

2353 Wt W2544/1454 700,000 5/15 D. D. & L. A.D.S.S./Forms/C. 2118.

WAR DIARY or INTELLIGENCE SUMMARY

Army Form C. 2118.

(Erase heading not required.)

Instructions regarding War Diaries and Intelligence Summaries are contained in F.S. Regs., Part II and the Staff Manual respectively. Title pages will be prepared in manuscript.

Place	Date	Hour	Summary of Events and Information	Remarks and references to Appendices
	1916 Dec 6		Lt Coy in Dispersions on the 5th inst — Casualties 20 OR wounded — Lewrin Normal	
	7th		" " " " " " — 2nd Lt G. Righy proceeded on leave — Counter Shell-cratered Normal — On the Evening the 10th Northumberland Fusiliers relieved the 9th Yks in the Line — Relief complete 7 p.m. — Lt Col Perry returned to Batt. marched to YPRES SIDING & entrained for East Cuming & 11 Bog. Hence by road to St LAWRENCE CAMP. — Arrived in Camp 12 Mid Night	
	8th		Bath at LAWRENCE CAMP. — 2nd Lt A. Wood proceeded on a Lewis gun Course Program of work was issued for the 9th to the 15th inst inclusive.	
	9th		Bath at LAWRENCE CAMP. — Fire occurred about 12-15 p.m. in Hut B 9 Officers Kit Bog and destroyed all Kits and damaged 30 Kit Bits. — A number of men taken during the day — Lt Lumford to Hospital sick — Capt C. Palmer retd from leave	
	10th		Bath at LAWRENCE CAMP — Church Parade in the morning — 2nd Lt Coore retd from Course of Instruction — 2nd Lt R Kerry proceeded on a Course at 23rd Div Schl — Capt. H. McBride retd from leave	
	11th		Bath at LAWRENCE CAMP. — 2nd Lt L.B. Chambers and 2nd Lt A.M. Peakman proceeded on leave.	
	12th		Bath at LAWRENCE CAMP. In the Evening a Concert was given by men of the Regiment. Great success	

2353 Wt. W2544/1454 700,000 5/15 D.D.&L. A.D.S.S./Forms/C.2118.

WAR DIARY
or
INTELLIGENCE SUMMARY.
(Erase heading not required.)

Army Form C. 2118.

Place	Date	Hour	Summary of Events and Information	Remarks and references to Appendices
	1916			
	Dec 13		Ord St Lawrence Camp - 2nd Batn arrived from Hospital	
	14th		G.O.C. Division inspected all R.C Machinery H Coy y 16 Batn and cleared C.Q.M.S. CLARKSON T. and Cpl. POSSINI E. - R.C. & C.P. were recommended for commission. Men inspected by F.I.C. at Brigade Headquarters - Punishments recognized there.	
	15th		R. Detn entrained at Civil Camp Siding for YPRES Siding and then marched to be Barracks and relieved the 8th YORKSHIRE Regt - Relief completed about 7 p.m.	
	16th		Bn at L.G. BARRACKS - Lt M HAMILTON returned to OC 71st Field Ambulance for X ray. Duty mobiles in going dental treatment - Capt A. DROUIN R.D.M.O. took over temporary medical charge of the Batn - Working party required estimate by 2 I.O. O.R.	
	17th 1 p.m.		Bn at L.G. BARRACKS - Church parades in the Morning - Divine service 8 p.m. Strength 28 Offrs 1000 O.R. Marches Barracks - Working party required as on 16th inst.	
	19th		Bn at L.G. BARRACKS - A.D.O.S. (Brill Stratwichi) inspected by G.O.C. at 10 a.m. Had Hat Sm for relieved in R.D. Recent Reviews in R. Line - Relief complete at 11:45 p.m. Inspection Party in Ypres Aug 3rd O Coy in right 3rd in front line A Coy in rear C Coy in platoon WELLINGTON St 1 plat in ATHOLL St 1 plat in RITZ St Offs & at the TUILLERIES - 2nd Wiltsreli from Front Course - 2nd W left with SM. Hand	

WAR DIARY or INTELLIGENCE SUMMARY

Army Form C. 2118.

Place	Date	Hour	Summary of Events and Information	Remarks and references to Appendices
	1916			
	Dec 20		Capt in Dugout in an eye of 19th inst – Situation Normal – Casualties Nil – Tim Rev Officer joined Bn at 5.a.m. 2nd Lt H. METZGER & LIEUT A.T. ELLISON – of 7th Tr.Mn. HUGHES Regt. from Lexington Grove – 2/2 Bn (CROWTHER & 2/2 Lt. TESTER proceed on leave	
	Dec 21		Bn in dugouts from 19th inst – Situation normal – Casualties 2/Lt F. DAVIS wounded in back 2 OR killed 2 OR wounded	
	Dec 22		Bn in dugouts on an 19th – Situation Normal – Casualties Nil – Medical Charge of the Battalion – Capt G. DROVIN RAMC on being relieved proceeded Fd. Amb Ambulance.	
	Dec 23		Bn in dugouts over 19th – The 9 The of L were relieved by 10/17th Br. Hussars at 2 a.m. and on relief moved to the BARRACKS YPRES arriving in Billets at 9.30 P.M.	
	Dec 24		Bn at R. BARRACKS – Everting parts supplied amounting of 173 OR	
	Dec 25		Bn at R. BARRACKS " " "	
	Dec 26		Bn at R. BARRACKS " " " 113 OR	
			2/Lt L.D. CHAMBERS appt Signalling Officer L/S LT A.T. ELLISON posted to Bomb Bn Gren 2/Lt HAWOOD appts Transport Officer – Epl Major DOBSON T. apptd WHITING S.M. were awarded by G.O.C Division at Reo. M Gr. (Military Medal)	

Army Form C. 2118.

WAR DIARY
or
INTELLIGENCE SUMMARY.
(Erase heading not required.)

Instructions regarding War Diaries and Intelligence Summaries are contained in F. S. Regs., Part II, and the Staff Manual respectively. Title pages will be prepared in manuscript.

Place	Date	Hour	Summary of Events and Information	Remarks and references to Appendices
	1916			
	Dec 27		Meal Kit Inspection – Working Parties supplied consisting of 447 OR. – Promenaders Nos 11 & 12 Relieved Fronts in the Line – Relief Complete about 7 p.m. – Dispositions B Coy in Tiger Trench C Coy on right 2nd from the Ypre Lowe Road – A Coy, 2/Lt Newington Crescent Ypre Font St. Ypre Maple St. KOY in R.I.L. St. Pytham in the Tuileries	
	28th		Rain throughout – No enemy action – Quiet on our front – Situation Normal – Casualties Nil	
	29th		Rain throughout noon – B.K. Evacuation Normal Casualties Nil – 2/Lt T M Peakman proceeded on Course of Instruction at Divisional School	
	30th		Rain throughout noon – 28th our Situation Normal Casualties Nil	
	31st		The 10th Northumberland Fusiliers relieved Bn. 9th F & S in the Line – After Relief Bttn. moved to YPRES SIDING and entrained for Earl Camp, arriving there by about 10 pm. in Billets at 12 midnight – Casualties Nil	

R Ratcliffe Lt Col.
Com 1st & 15 York & Lan. Regt.

4 JAN. 1917

WAR DIARY or INTELLIGENCE SUMMARY

Army Form C. 2118.

9th York & Lancs

Place	Date	Hour	Summary of Events and Information	Remarks and references to Appendices
	1917 Jan 1 to Jan 8		Cath at St Lawrence Camp - During this stay a satisfactory programme of work was carried out, including Hospital drill, Bayonet fighting, Guard duties, Musketry, Saluting drill etc. All men were medically inspected. 2nd Lt Scott and 2nd Lt Gunther with 12 men from 11th Res Capt AW Wilde joined the Bath and were in command of C Coy.	
	2nd		Jan 2nd was observed as Xmas day - 2nd Lt Wentworth from Lewis Gun Course	
	3rd		A number of men bathed at Poperinghe - Working parties consisting of 2 Officers + 270 OR were found - Lt AT Elliott with from Lewis Gun Course	
	4th		2nd Lt ET Radford proceeded on Divl Gas School Course	
	5th		Working parties consisting of 4 NCOs + 59 men were found	
	6th		Working parties consisting of 3 NCOs and 50 men were found. Church parade - Working party consisting of 2 Officers + 70 OR found - killed 1 2nd Lt AR Marker + 7 OR - wounded 30 OR killed 2 + no such casualties.	
	7th		2nd Lt JH Hughes proceeded on a Grenade Course - Working party of 2 NCO + 43 Men typical relief relieved the 9th Yorkshire Regt ACD Coys in the Bund "D" Coy in dugouts + Mr Intern'ts 30 at Manoloch dugouts at YPRES - Relief completed 10.45PM - Casualties 1 OR Wounded	

Army Form C. 2118.

WAR DIARY
or
INTELLIGENCE SUMMARY.
(Erase heading not required.)

Instructions regarding War Diaries and Intelligence Summaries are contained in F.S. Regs, Part II. and the Staff Manual respectively. Title pages will be prepared in manuscript.

Place	Date	Hour	Summary of Events and Information	Remarks and references to Appendices
	1917 Jan. 10th		Batt. C.O. on board the Cund - Working Parties of 2 Officers & 175 OR Supplied - Casualties 2 OR wounded. Dispositions as 9th - Working parties consisting of 20 Officers & 175 OR Supplied - 2 Lt Bagnall joined the Batt. & posted to A Coy - New Pioneer section inspected by G.O.C. arrived the Batt. Draft of 47 OR arrived.	
	11th		Dispositions as 9th - Working parties consisting of 2 Officers & 175 OR Supplied - 2 Lt Russell & 2 Lt Dermott & 2 Lt 773 Montagu returned from leave.	
	12th		Dispositions as 9th - Batt. relieved 11th Durham Fusiliers in the line and were 12/13th - Dispositions. A Coy on right support line, B Coy on left, C Coy in centre, D Coy in support, H.Q. Ruskin House. 2 Lt Hustand to Hospital - 2 Lt HH Raymond to Corps Training Camp & 2nd in Training New Dr...	
	13th		Dispositions as evening of 12th - Situation normal - Casualties 4 OR wounded	
	14th		Dispositions as 13th - Situation normal - Casualties Nil - 2 Lt 2 Davies proceeded to 2 Army School on Signal course	
	15th		Dispositions as 13th - Situation normal - Casualties Nil -	
	16th		Dispositions as 13th - Situation normal - Casualties 1 OR died of wounds - Hostile Artillery active - Relieved by 11th Rumored Fusiliers during night 16/17th - Dispositions 3 Coys at Helrund "C" Coy in Flagstaff St - 17th in New Dugouts at 9-15pm - 2 Lt Hughes etc from Leave	

WAR DIARY or INTELLIGENCE SUMMARY

Army Form C. 2118.

Place	Date	Hour	Summary of Events and Information	Remarks and references to Appendices
	1917			
	Jan 17		Disposition as evening of 16th inst – Working parts supplied consisting of 4 R.O.s & 67 men	
	18th		Disposition no 17th – Working parties consisting of 4 officers & 270 O.R. supplied.	
	19th		Disposition no 17th Working parties as 18th inst	
	20th		Batt. relieved 11th Shermut Foresters in the line – Relief complete 8 am. Disposition 3 Coys in left in front line "B" Coy in centre "D" Coy on right "C" Coy in support – "A" Coy in Ruckin Huts	
	21st		Coys in new disposition as coy of 20th – Situation Normal – Casualties Nil –	
	22nd		Disposition as 21st – Situation Normal – Casualties 1 OR Killed 1 OR Wounded – Hostile artillery intermittent[?] active throughout the day	
	23rd		Disposition as 21st – Situation Normal – Evacuation 1 OR Killed – 2 OR Wounded. General He Bastin K,L,M & Z platoons 97L – Relief complete 12-30 AM. On being relieved Coys moved	
	24th		to YPRES Raily. entrained for Cropoi Q.11 & g. thence to St Lawrence Camp Bois Camp at 3-30 am. 73rd man – Situation Normal – Casualties Nil – Batts at St Lawrence Camp – A programme of work was issued & carried out whilst the Batt. was in Camp	
	Jan 25 to Jan 31		On 26 " A lecture was given by Capt. Hutchinson R.F.A. on Wire Cutting 2 in Command & several other officers attended – Working parties supplied consisting of 1 Officer & 50 O.R.	

WAR DIARY
or
INTELLIGENCE SUMMARY.

Army Form C. 2118.

Place	Date	Hour	Summary of Events and Information	Remarks and references to Appendices
	1917 Jun 27		The G.O.C. inspected "D" Coy. - 2/Lt Dawnall proceeded on a bombing course	
	28th		Capt R.A Hislop asm Osborn proceeded to s/Army School for course of Instruction	
			Maj-Gen.g Weirs gave a lecture on the tactical handling of the Division	
			on MG's at Lozinghem Camp	
	29th		The C.O. inspected a B.C. Coys	
	31st		All Company were exercised in tactics for attack at Rifle School Marles Camp	

WAR DIARY or INTELLIGENCE SUMMARY

Army Form C. 2118.

ORDERLY ROOM 1 MAR 1917 6th BN. YORK & LANCASTER

Vol 15

Place	Date	Hour	Summary of Events and Information	Remarks and references to Appendices
	1917 Feb 1		Battn at Z Science Camp - Baths in use as usual	
	2		1st Yorks Regt relieved the Sherwood Foresters - about 7 pm relieved complete. Relief completed 7:30 pm	
	3		Battn in Reserve Brigade YPRES. Programme of Work carried out. Parts Casual-ments	
			Working parties supplied. Casualties 1 Officer and 1 OR.	
	4		Part of Batt in Reserve YPRES. Programme of work carried out - Working parts supplied no of workers	
			Relieved Notts & Derbys YPRES. Relief commenced ? pm - Working parts supplied 2 R.E. Battn - Relief to be completed ? pm	
			B.C.O. on Fire Belsis Rd Central. ? Winters parts no on 2nd night	
	5		Battn in B.G.D. YPRES - No to harass - No to move - Bath relieved NL second Brigade as garrison the front line	
			Preparation for the inspection. 5/Rep/ Corps Co. op in next times of Co. 2nd Division - 2nd Position S.	
			Co. 3rd LEINSTER Regt 1st Pos. 6 pm. Atty/Genl Hon 2 M M.O.E. Bn H.Q. HUE W/W Horse Huy. Umpire B.M.	
	6		Dispositions as opening of scheme. Relieved. Dinner. Casualties Nil	
	7		Dispositions as of man. Scheme. Dinner. Casualties 3 OR Wounded	
	8		Deposition as 6 mst. Scheme. Dinner. Casualties Nil -	
	9		Departures to the Cheshire Works Course in front - Mr Williams & HH Edwards - proceed to Bertrancourt to 5/Regt Opn	
	10		Field inspection Brooms YPRES. - Prognam of work sent to ? inspection - Boys the ? Band /Vies / GS.R Lt Rowatt Jones/ Op.	
	11		Preparation as 11th - Church parade 9:45 am. Regt Transports at 4:45 pm returned to Camp. Working parts 2 offices 200 OR supplied	

Army Form C. 2118.

WAR DIARY
or
INTELLIGENCE SUMMARY.
(Erase heading not required.)

Instructions regarding War Diaries and Intelligence Summaries are contained in F. S. Regs., Part II. and the Staff Manual respectively. Title pages will be prepared in manuscript.

Place	Date	Hour	Summary of Events and Information	Remarks and references to Appendices
	1917 Feb. 12.		An Inspection Parade at YPRES. — Capt Gillies & Lt Dunstan joined Unit. — Reference Reactional Sports Winter parts	
	13.		Outfitted on Horses — Beginning of WORK carried out. Rays as Staff Post all Men to O.Rs. Disposition of 1st ── Brunch on 11th Transport printed in Jan lens — Disposition of B Coy on Construction DLR 2nd Cdn Div. Reference 100 2nd Div Artist dt ── 2nd Leinster St ── B1 Rossignol St ── B1a Hoy Mondau── B1 Hoy Hay Day Ecr── Field Company &c.	
	14.		Dispositions for 15th ── as in 13th ── Situation Normal ── Casualties O.R. wounded.	
	15.		Dispositions as 14th ── Situation Normal ── Casualties 2 OR wounded.	
	16.		Disposition as 15th ── Situation Normal ── Casualties 2 OR wounded.	
	17.		Dispositions as 16th ── Situation Normal ── Casualties 1 OR ── 19th Hussars returned 9 P.M. in the evening ── 13th Hussars continue at YPRES.	
	18.		Sidney Attached Cecil Brown G.H.Q. Hence to PLOEGSTEERT camp — unit on coming 57779, 18th inst. Bn St Lawrence came At 4 & 11 A.M. to dinner with special Mission. — Remainder of Bn carried out Programme of Work not being Carry.	
	19.		Capt Stanley Attached to Engineer Canvas ── 2/B Platoon proceeded to No. 2 Field Survey Co. Army H.Q.	
	20.		Inspection of Unit by C.O.	
	21.		Root March — 211 men paraded who had not been in the March (Sun 13 Men) Route March — R.C.Ch. Church Parade & by Griffithcock —	
	22.		Lieut R. Ratcliffe Capt. L. Bate's joined 2nd WORCESTER Sangt Capt 7 Myor 749 were billeted took over Command of Battn. Capt. J. Power Toohey was 2nd Command ── Rifleman attached to Bar Battery ── Draft of 61 OR arrived	

2353 Wt. W2544/1454 700,000 5/15 D. D. & L. A.D.S.S./Forms/C. 2118.

Army Form C. 2118.

WAR DIARY
or
INTELLIGENCE SUMMARY.
(Erase heading not required.)

Instructions regarding War Diaries and Intelligence Summaries are contained in F. S. Regs., Part II. and the Staff Manual respectively. Title pages will be prepared in manuscript.

Place	Date	Hour	Summary of Events and Information	Remarks and references to Appendices
	1917 Feb 23		Route March	
			On Coy Training Camp at 12:30 PM entraining on Chinese Mortar Programme - Detrained at Bulle Zeele 2-13 PM	
	24		Marched to Millom - Bivouac Billets 4 PM	
	25		Bn Left Millom at 11-1 AM, marched & Boys at 8 AM - Bath in Billets 12-20 PM	
	26		On Left Paquegem at 10-15 AM, marched to Zouafques - Rest on Billets at 12-30 PM	
	27		On in Billets Zouafques - Coys at Disposal of O.C.Coys for Cleaning Billets Equipment &c. H.E. Occupied list	
	28		On in Billets at Zouafques - A.B.C Coys practiced under R.S.M. - Range X allotment Coys for practice. Showing finging scoring application - Capt Sumner took all Coys in fire instruction all Remainder under 2nd R/Lient, practiced to Range X for firing practice Syr allm practiced under the Signalling Officer	

Signed (illegible) Major
Commdg 9th York Lancaster Regt

Army Form C. 2118.

WAR DIARY
or
INTELLIGENCE SUMMARY.
(Erase heading not required.)

9th YORK & LANCS Vol 16

Place	Date	Hour	Summary of Events and Information	Remarks and references to Appendices
	1917 Mar 1 to Mar 18		Battalion in Billets at LOUVAQUES. Satisfactory programme of instruction issued which was most carefully carried out. This included Bayonet fighting, Bombing, Musketry, Extended order drill, Company drill, Platoon drill, Company & Battalion in attack etc - Lectures were given to all N.C.O. Men from time to time - On Mar 1 Rang. Ammo allotted to the Batt. from 8 p.m. to 12 noon & again on Mar 6th - On Mar 9 The B.n took part in the "Brigade Field day" Capt Dudley Lewis Joined the B.n on 10.3.17 H.O.T.T. were command. of D Coy, 2nd RTM LEAKEY Joined 10 inst. was posted to B Coy. Mar 11th Final of the Inter platoon Football Competition was played. Result Headquarters Hq. Girls No 3 Platoon 1 goal - C.S.M. DOBSON J.P. awarded the Italian Bronze Medal for Valour D.R.O. No 2496 of 11.3.17 - 2nd Lt L.B. CHAMBERS awarded Military Cross Auty D.R.O. 2492 of 9.3.17 x Capt wire No A/S.88 of 18.3.17 Mar 14th Semi Final of Brigade Inter pt Competition after 20 Minute extra play, Results 9th Y & L Regt 2 goals 8th Y & L Regt 0 goals Mar 17th The Batt. Lewis Gun B Coy marched to A Training Area carried out training scheme. The Batt. Cpt Billie. at 8 p.m. for myth Operators returning about 12 midnight 18 Coy E Service held on R.n Parade ground	

WAR DIARY or INTELLIGENCE SUMMARY

Army Form C. 2118.

Place	Date	Hour	Summary of Events and Information	Remarks and references to Appendices
	1917			
	Mar 8.		Final of Inter Plat Football Competition. Result 8 KOYLI v/s 9th Y+L. 0 goals.	
	" 19.		The Bn Left Billets at LOVAEGUES a Marched to BAYENGHEM arriving 12 noon.	
	" 20.		" " " " BAYENGHEM " " MILLAIN " 12 noon.	
	" 21.		" " " " MILLAIN " " HERZEELE " 4-30 p.m.	
	Mar 22 to 31st		Bn in Billets at HERZEELE. Programme of work carried and carried out. Mar 24th. Reconnaissance trips for all Officers NCOs. Subject Defence of a Village. 2nd Lt S.A. Edwards (SR) appointed Adjutant and to be Emp'd to whole as Emp'd gaz. vice Strugg. Capt M. Lewis (appre Brigade Major 112 Inf. Bde 8 Nov 1916. Cancld. 70 Supplmt Z.B. 765 d.23.3.17 Extract from List No 127 of Appointments. Commences 26/17 Mar 1917. Mar 26. First round Brigade Football Competition. Result. 11th Sherwood Foresters 6 goals. 9th York Lancs. 0 goals. — Mar 31st Co'ys Serve on B Coy Parade arrived. Mar 8. Inspection of 8th Bn 9th Bn YORK 'LANCASTER Regts on Football field by 102 Bde RFA. by the Army Commander. Mar 29th. 70th Bde Recreational training sports on "D" Coy 8 KOYLI Parade ground HOUTERQUE. Tug of War winners 9th Bn 'York Lancaster Regt - Cross Country Run (cancelled) Competition for Battalion Runners won by 9 Y L - Mr Ragnial Competition won by 9 Y L	

Army Form C. 2118.

WAR DIARY
or
INTELLIGENCE SUMMARY.
(Erase heading not required.)

Instructions regarding War Diaries and Intelligence Summaries are contained in F. S. Regs., Part II. and the Staff Manual respectively. Title pages will be prepared in manuscript.

Place	Date	Hour	Summary of Events and Information	Remarks and references to Appendices
	1917 Mar 29th		Extn. Coorts Competition Won by 5th KOYLI 2nd 9th Bn Y&L Regt. Transport Competition Won by 8th KOYLI 2nd 9th Bn Y&L Regt. Signalling Competition Won by 9th Y&L	
	Mar 30		Battalion Route March	
	31.		Afternoon Battalion Sports	

1-4-17

Arundel Major
Comdg 9th Bn York Lancaster Regt.

ORDERLY ROOM 1 APR 1917 9TH BN. YORK & LANCASTER REGT.

23

Army Form C. 2118.

WAR DIARY
or
INTELLIGENCE SUMMARY.
(Erase heading not required.)

9th Bn. York & Lancaster Regt.

Place	Date	Hour	Summary of Events and Information	Remarks and references to Appendices
	1917 April 1		Bat[talio]n in Billets at HERZEELE. A C[om]p[an]y. Church parade & worked on A C[om]p[an]y. parade ground. Major R. C. Middleton joined the Batt[alio]n and took over temp[orar]y Command during the absence of Col. Stones Wilson on Leave.	
	2nd		Bn. at HERZEELE. Church and Batt[alion]y. Pay. Battery. Programme of work: 2nd H. Park joined the Batt[alio]n on 3rd inst.	
	4th Apl		and C.O. No 21 was received on 4th inst.	
	5th & 6th		Batt. marched to OTTAWA CAMP near OUDERDOM during in Camp at 6 P.M. — B[attalio]n relieved the 12th Sussex Regt. in the Line. The Camp was L.C.P at 7 P.M. and B[attalio]n marched to VLAMERTINGHE Ry. Siding where it entrained for YPRES and thence to following disposition: D Coy on right from I.29 & Living Trench I.30.5 "C" Coy on the Left from I.30.5.b. St PETER ST. "B" Coy in HALIFAX ST. & "A" Coy in STAFFORD ST. with Batt. H.Q.rs at RUSKIN HOUSE — Relief was completed by 2 A.M. of 7 inst with no Casualties Batt. in same disposition	
	7th & 8th			
	9th		at 6 A.M on 9th inst the Enemy commenced systematic Bombardment of our wire & trenches which he kept up throughout the day — At 6.30 P.M. the Bombardment became intense & at 7.30 P.M. was lifted on to our supports & the enemy attacked on a wide Battalion front. This Rifles engaged our own Company, the L.C.Ss. in advance	

Army Form C. 2118.

WAR DIARY
or
INTELLIGENCE SUMMARY.
(Erase heading not required.)

Instructions regarding War Diaries and Intelligence Summaries are contained in F. S. Regs., Part II. and the Staff Manual respectively. Title pages will be prepared in manuscript.

Place	Date	Hour	Summary of Events and Information	Remarks and references to Appendices
	1917 Apr 9		up and our Lewis Guns were brought to bear upon the enemy. He endeavoured in forming a party in our trench but was quickly driven out by Lewis Gun fire from the flank. Bomb stores and 2 prisoners in our trenches	
	11th		The Batt: was relieved by the 8th K.O.Y.L.I. and went into Bivouac Reserve at RAILWAY DUGOUTS. — Total casualties during the tour 12 KILLED 44 WOUNDED	
	8th		Capt. F.T. POWER proceeded to England. Daily C.R. No 57340 of 3.4.17	
	12/13th		Batt: at KNIGHT DUGOUTS. Working Parties of 4 Officers and 333 O.R. furnished daily	
	14/15th Night		Bn relieved the 9th YORKSHIRE REGT. and proceeded by Rue Maud to OTTAWA CAMP. arriving in Camp at 3am 15-4-17 mon	
	17th		T.G.O.C. inspected the Batt: at 11am and congratulated them on Reinford work during their recent tour in the trenches. H.G. & Coys proceeded to ZWEBEKE Burd to supply Working Parties	
	1st R.		Lt Col J.H. BONES WILSON proceeded to 2nd Army Hqs. - Lt R.E. WILSON MC joined the Batt.	
	18th		The G.O.C. Division inspected No 14 Platoon AB Coy on returned to OTTAWA Camp	
	21st		2nd Lt. F. CAPLESS & 2nd Lt M. PROCTER joined the Batt. Lt Col J.H. BONES WILSON Returned to Batt.	

2353 Wt. W2544/1454 700,000 5/15 D.D.&L. A.D.S.S./Forms/C. 2118.

WAR DIARY or INTELLIGENCE SUMMARY

Army Form C. 2118.

Place	Date	Hour	Summary of Events and Information	Remarks and references to Appendices
	1917			
	22/23	11.30pm	Batt relieved 8th Yorkshire Regt at RAILWAY DUGOUTS. Relief carried out by Route March from OTTAWA CAMP - Relief complete 11-30 pm 22.4.17	
	23-25th		Batt in reserve at RAILWAY DUGOUTS – Working Parties of 6 Officers & 275 OR supplied daily	
	26/27th		Batt relieved the 1 R.S.F. in the Line. MINDY CORNER to RAILWAY CUTTING. I. 34. d. I.2. I. 35. I. "C" Coy in support SONNEN Rd. & "D" Coy in support SONNEN Rd. Supplied Carrying "A" Coy on left "B" Coy on right. Batth HQ in SP9 Batth HQ10. SP9. Relief complete 10-30 pm.	
	27th		In same disposition – 2nd Lt ST. BREINGAN joined the Batth & posted to "D" Coy. Casualties 3 OR Wounded	
	28th		In same disposition. Casualties 6 OR wounded (1 since died)	
	29th		Same disposition. Casualties nil	
	30th		Same disposition. Casualties nil On 30th OR No 27 received	
			In connection with Enemy raid on 90th Bde the following awards were allotted to Bn.	
			Lt C. PALMER MILITARY CROSS	
			2nd Lt A.A. DENYER MILITARY CROSS	
			No 34095 Sgt S. FORBES D.C.M.	
			- 9223 Sgt J.W. MANN D.C.M.	
			3. OR MILITARY MEDALS & 5 Certificates of Award for Valour	

Comm'd'g 2 York & Lancaster Regt

WAR DIARY or INTELLIGENCE SUMMARY

Army Form C. 2118.

Vol 18

Place	Date	Hour	Summary of Events and Information	Remarks and references to Appendices
	1917 May 1st		Bn in the line WINDY CORNER to RAILWAY CUTTING. I.34.b, I.35.1, I.35.2. A Coy in left, B on right C Coy in support SUNKEN RD. D Coy in reserve S.P.9. Bn Hqrs S.P.9. On the night of 2/3 the battalion was relieved by the 1/5 Warwicks Regt. The Battalion moved to billets 3 kilometres W of POPERINGHE, Bn Hqrs at G.11.a.2.3.	
	May 3-9th		Bn carried out satisfactory company training on the training ground of the 55th Division and field operations on the BOESCHAPE Training area.	
	May 10th		Bn marched to ST LAWRENCE camp near BRANDHOEK	
	May 11th		On the night of 11/12th the battalion relieved the 10th Welsh Regt in the line. The camp was left at 9pm & marched to BRANDHOEK siding where the battalion entrained for ypres and thence to following dispositions. C Coy on left from BIRR X roads to left of 3 GAP. D Coy BOND ST locality. B Coy in support in WELLINGTON CRESCENT & A Coy in reserve at HALFWAY HO. (Bn Hqrs) Relief was complete by 2.30am with no casualties. Bn Scouts dispositions	
	May 12,13th May 13th		On night of 13th/14th the battalion was relieved by the 1st East Surrey Regt and entrained at YPRES for POPERINGHE & thence marched to the same billets as it occupied from May 3rd to 9th.	
	May 14,15,17,18th 21st + 22nd		Bn practised offensive from MT SORREL system on a flag course situated on the BOESCHEPE Training area.	

Army Form C. 2118.

WAR DIARY
or
INTELLIGENCE SUMMARY.
(Erase heading not required.)

Place	Date	Hour	Summary of Events and Information	Remarks and references to Appendices
	May 21st		The Bn Hqrs mess entertained four nurses of the 3rd Canadian C.C.S. to tea.	
	May 24th		2/Lt Bunce S.K. joined the bn and was posted to D Coy.	
			On the night of 24th/25th the bn was entrained at POPERINGHE for YPRES where it relieved the 9th Yorkshire regiment in the following dispositions. B Coy left front line from ST PETERS ST to SAP F. C Coy right front coy from SAP F to L.30.a. D Coy in support at HALIFAX ST & A Coy in reserve at MAPLE TR. Bn Hqrs at RUDKIN Ho.	
	May 26th		D Coy Hqrs dugout blown in about 5.30 am. 2/Lt Bruce S.K. & 2/Lt Potter M. & 2/Lt Breingan S.K. were killed.	
	May 27th		On the night of 27th/28th the bn was relieved by the 11th Bn Sherwood Foresters. The Bn took over billets as follows. A, B & D Coys in RAILWAY DUGOUTS & C Coy 9 Bn Hqs at BUND.	
	May 29th		The orderly room was blown in by a 5.9" shell about 6 pm and all records and papers were destroyed.	
	May 31st		On the night of 31st/1st the bn was relieved by the 12th D.L.I. regt & marched via KRUISTRAAT HOEK to bivouacs at _____ Total casualties this tour O.R. 4 killed, 24 wounded. J. Howden-Hm	
			1 wounded. 2 killed	
			Others	

J.H.R.
Commdg 9 Yorkshires

Army Form C. 2118.

WAR DIARY
or
INTELLIGENCE SUMMARY.
(Erase heading not required.)

9th Bn. YORK AND LANCS. REGT.

No. G.26. Date 2.7.17

Vol 19

Place	Date	Hour	Summary of Events and Information	Remarks and references to Appendices
	June 1st		BUND Bn was relieved in the early morning in the Bund line by the 12th DLI. There were two casualties on the way to camp owing to enemy shelling back areas with gas shells. The Bn arrived in P camp at 3.30 a.m., but moved on the evening to bivouacs at S.24.b.4.5.	
S.24.b.4.5	June 2nd to June 5th		Bn at S.24.b.4.5. Coys were inspected by the C.O. & thorough organisation of coys for the coming Offensive was carried out.	
	June 5th		On the evening of the 5th the Bn moved via Vlamertinghe, Kruystraat to the N end of BUND to the following dispositions. Bn H.Q. HALFWAY Ho., A,B & C Coys WELLINGTON CRESCENT, D Coy MAPLE TR.	
	June 6th		On the evening of the 6th Bn moved to assembly positions previous to the attack. Bn front being from N end of CANADA ST. to N end of B front line. There were no casualties whilst the Bn was assembling.	
	June 7th		At 3.10 a.m. (zero hour) our artillery opened up a terrific barrage on the Hun front line & simultaneously the mines under Hill 60 and the CATERPILLAR were blown. At zero +1 the first wave consisting of B Coy on the right & A Coy on the left (A Coy in support at short intervals). The attack progressed very favourably and by zero + 30	

Place	Date	Hour	Summary of Events and Information	Remarks and references to Appendices
June 4th			the Bn had reached the objective and begun consolidating. Very few casualties were sustained in the actual attack at 3.00 + 3h 40mm the 8th Bn York's Lancaster Bn & the 8th Bn KOYLI on the right & left respectively went over from our objective and reached the final objective of the Brigade.	
	June 9th		The Bn remained in the objectives until the evening of the 9th. During this period the Bn underwent heavy shelling & sustained many casualties. B Coy also relieved the 8th Bn YorL in the front line on the morning of the 9th. On the evening of the 9th the Bn was relieved by the 1st N. Staffs Bn. The Total casualties sustained were Officers - killed 4 (including the C.O.) wounded 6. O.Rs - killed 39. wounded 211. Died of wounds 9. missing 18.	
	Nyt 9th/9th/10th June 10th 11th		On relief the Bn moved by motor lorries from KRUISTRAAT to SCOTTISH LINES Capt D Rennie TooR over Temp command of Bn, following on Lt Col Bowes Wilson, killed in action 9.6.14. Coys at OSC Coys disposal for cleaning up & re-organisation	
	June 12th		The G.O.C Div. inspected Bn in the morning. Sgt Wright D.C.M was decorated after inspection Bn marched to billets at METEREN, arriving in billets by 4.30 p.m.	

WAR DIARY / INTELLIGENCE SUMMARY

Army Form C. 2118.

Place	Date	Hour	Summary of Events and Information	Remarks and references to Appendices
	June 12th		Capt S.W. brooks rejoined the Bn. W.E.F. & took over command of C Coy	
	13th		Bn in billets at METEREN. The usual courses on Bn parade ground	
	to 25th		were allotted to Coys. Special attention was paid to specialists. On the	
			19th the Range near St KOYLI was allotted to Coys.	
	20th		Bde bombing competition - Result 9 & 4 plt 2 3 pts first.	
			2 plts Anglia O.W. Wilson R joined the Bn	
	22nd		18 Corps Rifle camps were placed at the disposal of Coys.	
	25th		Capt Sykes O.W. joined the Bn & was posted to A Coy	
	26th		Bn moved by march route from METEREN to camp at La CLYTE about J.36.C.4.	
			Leaving METEREN at 6.45 am & arriving in camp at 12 noon.	
	27th		Bn relieved the 12th Bn R.F's in the line. Bn H.Q. HEDGE ST Tunnels	
			D Coy on left from I.30.b.5y to I.30.d.3.0.95 B Coy on right from I.30.d.2.5	
	to		C Coy in reserve in HEDGE ST Tunnels & B Coy in support in CANADA ST	
	30th		Situation normal. Casualties Officers - 2 Officers killed, one wounded	
	28th to 30th		O.R. 2 killed, 1 died of wounds, 12 wounded.	

Copy No 5

The 9th Bn York's Lancaster Regiment.

OPERATION ORDER No 2
by
Lieut-Colonel J H Bowes-Wilson, Commanding.

Ref. Map 1/5,000. Div Map German Trenches.

1. **Intention.**
   In conjunction with an attack by the Rest of the 2nd Army, the 23rd Division will assault the German Trenches round HILL 60. & MOUNT SORREL.
   The 70th Brigade will be the left of the Second Army & forms a defensive flank. The 69th Infantry Brigade attacks on the right of the 70th Infantry Brigade. The Dividing line is shewn on the maps which have already been issued, as is also the objective, which is to be consolidated.

2. **Distribution of Bns. of the 70th Inf Bde**

   The Brigade will attack with two Battalions in the front line & two in Support.
   9th York & Lancs Regt. 'A' or Right Front attacking Battn.
   Bn H.Q. CANADA STREET

11th Sherwood Foresters. 'B' or Left front attacking Battn.
Bn. H.Q. HEDGE ST.

8th York & Lancs Regt. "C" or Right Support Bn
Bn. H.Q. CANADA ST.

8th Kings Own Yorkshire L.I. 'D' or Left Support Bn.
Bn. H.Q. SEBA Dug outs.

3. Dividing Line between A & B Bns
―――――――――――――――――――――

(a) In our front line -
The junction of the N. end of CANADA ST. & the front line.

(b) In German line - I 30. a. 87. 06 to trench junction I. 30. d. 20. 55. in attacking Bn Objective IMAGE LANE being inclusive to 'B' battalion.

4 Positions at ZERO – 2 hours
The Bn. will take up the following Positions in readiness to advance to the attack.
In front line starting from N. end of CANADA ST to end of our line, platoons

assembled in following order:-
7. 16. 5. 15. 2. 14. 1. 13.
In CANADA ST.
  Nos 8. 12. 11. Platoons.
In new trench behind front line.
  No 6. 9. 4. 10. 3.
Carrying Parties in trench leading
to GAP from CANADA ST.

5 <u>Movement in Assembly Positions.</u>
  <u>Order of March as follows:-</u>
     13   Platoon
      1   "
     14   "
      2   "
     15   "
      5   "
     16   "
      7   "
      3   "
     10   "
      4   "
      9   "
      6   "
     11   "
     12   "
      8   "
  Carrying Parties.

6. Barrages – Times – Method & order of Advance.

At ZERO Mines under HILL 60 & the CATERPILLAR will be fired.

18 pounders will barrage the enemy front line. Between I. 30. C. 55. 80. & I. 30. b. 05. 10 the barrage will be put about 50 yards behind the enemy front line.
Stokes mortars will barrage the enemy front line from about I. 30. C. 40. 80 to the left.

ZERO +1. Barrage lifts (except on IMMEDIATE Trench on its right to I. 30. C. 30. 70.) & will move slowly back allowing for a pace of 25 yards a minute.

ZERO + **9**. Barrage on **IMMEDIATE** Trench will lift conform to the remainder of the barrage

ZERO + 20. Barrage lifts off Battalion objective & will pause about 200 yards in front of this line till ZERO plus 3 hours 40 minutes.

ZERO + 3 hours. Barrage again lifts 4/3 & allows C & D 40 minutes. BNS. to advance to take their objective.

At ZERO + 1. A & B Companies will advance two platoons in two lines forming the 1st wave – Distance between lines 15 yards.

This first wave will be followed by D Company the Moppers-up in one line. Next the 2nd wave of A & B Companies two platoons in two lines. The distance between the 1st & 2nd wave must not be more than 100ˣ.

C Company forming the 3rd wave will follow across "NO MAN'S LAND" in lines of sections in file keeping this formation as long as practical. This 3rd wave not to be more than 100ˣ from the 2nd wave.

7. <u>Company objectives.</u>
A Company will capture the BN. objective between points I.30.C.40.00. inclusive to point I.30.C.8.3 exclusive.

OC A Coy. will at once establish blocks in IMPARTIAL LANE & new trench running into objective at point about I.30.C.60.05., & in IMAGE AVENUE.

6

Endeavours should be made to form one block at point where new trench cuts IMAGE AVENUE. He must take steps to safeguard his right flank as the West Yorkshire Regiment, the left attacking battalion of the 69th Brigade are not timed to reach point I.30.c.40.00. till ZERO + 35 minutes.

B Company will capture objective from I.30.C.8.3. inclusive to trench junction I.30.d.20.55. establishing any necessary blocks.

D Company, the Moppers up(less two sections Lewis gunners in Battalion reserve) will be responsible for the mopping up of the MOUNT SORREL system in accordance with plans arranged.

C Company will leave one platoon, No 10, in enemy front line about point I.30.C.5.8. This platoon will bomb along IMMEDIATE trench directly barrage lifts at ZERO + 9. & gain touch with the West Yorkshire Regiment of the 69th Brigade.

7.

After gaining touch this platoon will advance through the wood to its front & join up with No 9. platoon in IMMEDIATE SUPPORT.
No 9. Platoon will go direct to IMMEDIATE support in close support of A Company.
Nos 12 & 11 platoons will take up position between points I.30.c.7.5 & I.30.d.1.5. near the road forming a close support to B Company.
If necessary the O.C. 'C' Company must push on to the Bn objective to help A & B Companies to gain this.

8. Consolidation

Immediately the Bn objective has been gained a line in or in front of this must be consolidated.
A support line must also be formed from the junction IMAGE ROW, IMAGE RESERVE. I.30.c.80.30 to junction of IMAGE LANE & IMAGE SUPPORT I.30.c.95.80. The platoon of C in support to B will commence this consolidation.
~~T~~ Lines must be firestepped & organised to resist counter attacks. Wiring to be commenced as soon as possible.

9. Machine Guns. 1 Section, 70th Machine Gun Company is allotted to the battalion. After the Bn. objective has been captured these guns will take up positions in the captured trenches in support of the battalion.

10. Strong Points.
Two are to be constructed in the Battalion area "G" S.P. at about point I.36.a.7.8. & "H" S.P. about I.30.C.60.35. The former will be made by A Company & on completion will be manned by A Company – Strength of garrison 20 rifles & 1 Lewis Gun. The latter will be constructed by R.E. & pioneers & manned by "C" Company – garrison as for "G".

11. Trench Mortars.
Three mortars & teams are allotted to the battalion. These assemble in CANADA ST. dug-out & on the battalion objective being captured, will move up & take positions in the captured trenches in support of the battalion. After the capture of their objectives by C & D Bns. these guns will move forward again – two in support of 'C' Bn, one in support of D Bn.

In every case reconnoitring parties will go forward with the last wave to select positions for these guns.

12. <u>Forward Communications</u>
Communication trenches across "No Man's Land" will be constructed by the R.E. as follows
  (a) From about I.30.c.4.9
  (b) From junction I.30.3. I.30.4.

13. <u>Contact Patrol.</u> A Contact Aeroplane will be up from ZERO (if light enough) until six hours after ZERO. Separate instructions are issued concerning this.

14. <u>Medical</u> Position of Regimental Medical Officers of the Brigade
A & C BNS SOUTH REGIMENTAL AID POST - MAPLE TRENCH I.24.c.3.7.
'B' BN NORTH REGIMENTAL AID POST
    I.24.c.3.8.
'D' BN With his Headquarters in SEBA Dug out

10

Advanced Dressing Station - ZILLEBEKE
BUND I 15. D. 1. 3.
Divisional Collecting Station - LILLE GATE

Route for wounded - Both stretcher &
walking cases to Regimental Aid
Post via track from front line to
MAPLE ST., - thence via Route C to
advanced dressing station
ZILLEBEKE BUND.
No one must fall out to help wounded.
All efforts must be concentrated on
attaining the objective.
Wounded will be cared for by
Stretcher Bearers whose number
has been increased.
15. Bⁿ Instructions. Separate
instructions are being issued.
(1) Fighting Kit.   (6) Instructions for
(2) Signalling.   moppers up.
(3) Contact aeroplanes.
(4) Rations.
(5) Dumps affecting the Bⁿ
These & any others that may be issued
must be read in conjunction
with these orders.

16th Bn. Headquarters   11.

   CANADA ST. till situation
is clear. Afterwards near
point I.30.c.6.6. Move will
be notified to all companies.

                      3-6-17   Geo. A. Gunther Lt+Adj.
Copies issued to   9 Y.L.
  No. 1   File
  Nos 2 to 5.   O.C. Coys.
  No 6   70 Inf Bde
  No 7   11th Sherwood Foresters

Instructions No. 10   Nominal Rolls

O.C. Coys & the R.S.M. will forward a complete nominal roll of all Officers, N.C.O's & men who are proceeding to the trenches on X Y night. This roll to reach Bn Orderly Room one hour before the Battalion moves off.

All Section, platoon & Company Commanders will have in their possession a nominal roll of their sections, platoons & Companys respectively, corrected accordingly.

All the above rolls to be carefully checked on arrival in the trenches on X night & any alterations to be reported to Bn. HQS immediately.

A revised nominal roll will be forwarded to Bn. H.S. in duplicate by Companies on taking their positions for assault.

All Officers will also be in possession of a roll of their Coy who are proceeding to the trenches.

The R.S.M. and Co. Sgt Majors will keep nominal rolls of all N.C.O.s & men who are staying behind at the Transport lines.

G. Alquerster Lt Maj
9th

3/6/17

Instructions No 2

Signalling

Communication

Prior to the capture of the BN objective and until such time as Brigade forward Station is established communication will be maintained by runner to BN HQS in CANADA ST.

After capture of the BN objective a Brigade Forward station will be established in a dugout about point I 30. c 6.6. This forward Station will be the centre of communication for all companies and will transmit messages by the best means available at the time.

A Coy will establish a visual Stn as near to I. 30. c. 3. 0. as is convenient working with Lucas daylight lamp & shutter to RUDKIN HOUSE & Brigade Forward Stn. Two pigeons will also be carried.

"B" Co. will establish a visual
Stn. at I.30.d.2.3. working
with shutter to Bois forward
Stn.

C & D Coy's will when possible
communicate by visual to
RUDKIN HSE. or Brigade forward
Stn.
RUDKIN HOUSE is visible from
I.30.c.3.3

Communication from Coys to
platoons will be by Runner
only

NOTE.
Runners must work in pairs
taking the same Route, one
following the other up about
50 yds. Messages to be carried in
right hand top pocket of
tunic.

3/6/17

C.W. Gunther Lt. Maj.
9YZ

F. 70

Instructions No 3. — Contact Aeroplane

(1) The contact aeroplane mentioned in Operation Order No. 2. para 13. will be distinguished by three broad white bands on the fuselage & by the attachment of a black board on the left lower plane. This contact aeroplane will call for flares by firing a white light & sounding a Klaxon horn. Leading infantry will light flares approximately at the following times —

ZERO + 30 minutes
 "   " 1 hour
 "   " 4 hours 30 minutes
 "   " 5 hours.

Infantry must however ensure that the aeroplane is calling for flares before lighting up.
It is recognised that in confused fighting it is difficult for bodies of troops to know if they are actually the leading troops & it must not be assumed that flares show that there are no other troops in front.
Isolated bodies out of touch on their flanks should light

2.

flares when called on to do so. The colour of the flares issued are green.

(3) A wireless aeroplane will be up throughout the day for the purpose of looking out for counter attacks. A red light fired from this aeroplane will denote an impending counter attack N of the canal. The position & direction of enemy movement will be communicated by this plane through the Artillery to the Brigadier concerned who will warn Battalion Commanders concerned.

<u>Note</u>. Flares must be lighted in threes. Single flares are difficult for the aeroplane to see. Matches for lighting of these to be carried.

5/6/17

Callgainten Lt Col
9 Y L

F. 40

Moppers Up.

Ref. Operation Order No 2. for the coming offensive, Para 6.

The following amendments will be made:-

Every other man detailed as a Mopper Up will carry two flags as under :-

    1 RED
    1 BLUE

Dug-outs which have been cleared & into which no M.S.K. or 'P' Bomb has been thrown will be marked with a BLUE Flag.

Dug-outs into which an M.S.K. or 'P' Bomb has been thrown will be marked with a RED Flag & a sentry will be posted at each entrance.

5/6/17

G.A.Gunther Lt Col
9.y.z

F. 71

Instructions No 4. – Rations.

Day of Consumption.	Drawn.	Remarks.
X.	Normally in Camp	—
Y.	Normally	Carried up with Battn. in men's haversacks.
Z.	Now at Q.M Stores.	Carried up with Battn. on X/Y on pack animals.
A	Brigade Dump ZILLEBEKE. House immediately next Churchyard Gate.	Bacon & cheese rations for A day at present at Q.M Stores. These will be dumped at ZILLEBEKE on night X/Y. Remainder of rations already dumped.
B	Normally	

Note. Bacon rations for Y, Z & A days will be cooked in Camp before issue.

5/6/17

C.A.Gunther Lt Col
9??

1/4/548
" 5"
9" York & Lancs Regt

VOL 20

Army Form C. 2118.

WAR DIARY
or
INTELLIGENCE SUMMARY.
(Erase heading not required.)

Instructions regarding War Diaries and Intelligence Summaries are contained in F. S. Regs., Part II. and the Staff Manual respectively. Title pages will be prepared in manuscript.

Place	Date	Hour	Summary of Events and Information	Remarks and references to Appendices
LINE	July 1st		The battalion was relieved on the line by 11th Sherwood Foresters. On relief Bn. moved to MICMAC Camp H.32.c.5.5, arriving there about 6am on the morning of the 2nd.	
	2nd 8.00		2 Lieuts Pease J.H, Meikle D.H, Pennant & Stevenson R. & Mell J.E. - Thompson E.H joined the Bn on the 2.7.17.	
	3rd to 5th		Bn at MICMAC Camp. Satisfactory training was carried out. 7 coys reorganised on the 4 platoon basis.	
	4th		On the 4th ind. H.M the King passed HALLEBAST CORNER about 9.15 am. The Bn collected informally by the roadside to cheer the King. 2/Lt R Angles & J. La Page - a draft of 25 O.R's joined the Bn on the 4/7/17. B Coy & 95 O.R's of C Coy proceeded to BATTERSEA Fm on the W.M for work for 2 days.	
	5th		The 12th D.L.I relieved the Bn on the 5th. Coys dispose of the camp at I.32.b.4.5. The G.O.C inspected men of new draft on the 5th.	
	7th		The Bn less Bn. H.Q moved to the lines on the night of the 7/8 10pm to work under supervision of R.E's completing the work on the night of 8/7/17.	Hamlye Capt/A&tn 4.8.17

2353 Wt. W2544/1454 700,000 5/15 D.D.&L. A.D.S.S./Forms/C. 2118.

WAR DIARY or INTELLIGENCE SUMMARY

Army Form C. 2118.

Place	Date	Hour	Summary of Events and Information	Remarks and references to Appendices
	JULY			
	8th		Lt. Col. S.D Rumbold M.C. took over command of the Bn from the 8/7/14	
	14th		2Lts A.J Walton & C Asch joined the Bn on the 14/7/14	
	14th		The Bn moved to billets in the STEENVOORDE area by motor lorry arriving in billets about 5 p.m. Bn HQs K20 c.10.3.	
	15th		2Lt Senruba H.S. & a draft of 24 O.Rs joined the Bn.	
	15-17th		Bn carried out satisfactory training. On the 16th A & C coys marched to 8th KOYLI HQs for bayonet fighting over a specially prepared course.	
	18th		The Bn moved to the METEREN area on the 18th by march route, arriving in billets by 4 p.m. Bn H.Q. X 10 c. 3.4.	
	18th-31st		Whilst in the METEREN area satisfactory training programmes were carried out, including Assault Course, range practices, bayonet fighting, Musketry, section & platoon training as laid down in S.S.142. Bgn Carpenter drill, signal, platoon, coy & ceremonial drill.	
	24th		Bn sports were held on the 24th on the Bn parade ground at X.9.6.9.4. the G.O.C. presented the prizes	
	23rd		The G.O.C. Division inspected the Bn on the field at X.9.6.9.4.	

Army Form C. 2118.

WAR DIARY
or
INTELLIGENCE SUMMARY.
(Erase heading not required.)

Instructions regarding War Diaries and Intelligence Summaries are contained in F.S. Regs., Part II. and the Staff Manual respectively. Title pages will be prepared in manuscript.

Place	Date	Hour	Summary of Events and Information	Remarks and references to Appendices
METEREN	August 1st to 5th		The Batln in billets in the METEREN area. Training continued	
	3rd		Bn Route march with advance & rear guards	
	4th		All ranks have their S.B.R.'s tested & fitted under supervision of M.O.	
	6th		Bn left the METEREN area at 11 am & marched to CAESTRE & entrained for ARQUES, then by march route to camp 1 mile N of ARQUES. Bn reached camp at 7.15 pm.	
ARQUES. ALQUINES	7th		Bn left ARQUES at 10 am & marched to billets in ALQUINES. Journey away there by 7 pm. Bn remained here until 9th and	
	9th		Bn left the ALQUINES area at 9.45 am & marched to billets in NORTLEULINGHEM arriving in billets by 1 pm.	
NORTLEULINGHEM	10th		Bn left NORTLEULINGHEM at 4.30 pm and marched to WATTEN Station entraining at 12.45 am on the 11th for PROVEN, thence by march route to Tunnelling camp at ST JANSTER BEIZEN. Bn reached camp by 8.30 am.	
ST JANSTER BEIZEN.	11th to 12th 23rd		Bn at Tunnelling camp. Programme of work were issued & carried out - including artillery formation, Ceremonial drill, tactical digging and company training. Specialists received careful attention. Bn left camp at 5 am & marched to DOMINION Camp arriving at 11.15	

2353 Wt. W2544/1454 700,000 5/15 D.D.&L. A.D.S.S./Forms/C. 2118.

Army Form C. 2118.

WAR DIARY
or
INTELLIGENCE SUMMARY.

(Erase heading not required.)

Instructions regarding War Diaries and Intelligence Summaries are contained in F. S. Regs., Part II. and the Staff Manual respectively. Title pages will be prepared in manuscript.

Place	Date	Hour	Summary of Events and Information	Remarks and references to Appendices
	Aug.			
DOMINION CAMP.	24th		Bn in camp. Thorough inspection of platoons carried out by platoon commanders.	
CHATEAU SEGARD.	25th		The Bn less transport & details left behind moved to Chateau Segard by motor lorries, leaving camp at 2.30 pm & arriving at destination at 5 pm	
	26th		Bn at CHATEAU SEGARD.	
	27th		Bn left CHATEAU SEGARD at 6 pm & marched by companies to ZILLEBEKE BUND, arriving there at 8 pm.	
ZILLEBEKE BUND	28th & 29th		Bn in Bugade reserve at ZILLEBEKE BUND	
	30th		Bn relieved by 4th Bn. The Bn left ZILLEBEKE BUND at 6.45 pm & marched to the ASYLUM YPRES. Thence by motor lorries to WIPPENHOEK area. Bn arrived in camp at K 30 C.3.0. about 10 pm	
K 30. C. 30.	31st		Bn in camp at K 30 C.3.0.	

S.D. Rowley Col
Comdy ? ? ? ?

WAR DIARY or INTELLIGENCE SUMMARY.

Army Form C. 2118.

Vol 22

Place	Date	Hour	Summary of Events and Information	Remarks and references to Appendices
WIPPENHOEK	SEPTEMBER 1st & 2nd		Batt. under canvas in WIPPENHOEK AREA K 30 c 3.0.	
	3rd	8 a.m.	Left for NORTPEENE AREA by march-route thro' STEENVORDE, OXELEPE, BAYINCHOVE	
OOSTHOEK			arrived in billets at OOSTHOEK at 6 p.m.	
	4th to 11th		Batt at OOSTHOEK. Training was carried out which included bombing, musketry, bayonet fighting, practice formation for the attack, a flag course, coy drill, etc. Special training 7 to 10-	
	12th		Moved to LOYTRENE area at 2.15 p.m. arr. 5 p.m.	
	13	11 a.m.	STEENVORDE area (east), arrived billets 5.30 p.m.	
	14		Moved 6 a.m. to DICKEBUSCH area, arrived camp 3 p.m.	
	15		Relieved 8th BUFFS in N. subsector of civil front, relief complete about 7 p.m. dispositions: Bn. H.Q. C Coy & D Coy, HEDGE ST TUNNELS, B Coy on left, A Coy in JAM SUPPORT A Coy in night BODMIN COPSE.	
	17/18		Relieved by 15th HANTS & 8th ROYL: Batt moved to RAILWAY DUG-OUTS & became batt in reserve: afternoon of 18th to No 1 DICKEBUSCH area.	
	19		Moved fm camp at 9.45 p.m. to BEDFORD HOUSE being "A" Bth of Reserve Brigade	
	20		ATTACK DAY: at zero hour 5.40 a.m. Batt moved by platoons to TOR TOP & came into line 3 Coys + Batt H.Q. on TOR TOP 7.30 a.m. A Coy lost 22 killed & wounded. Fairly quiet day.	

WAR DIARY or INTELLIGENCE SUMMARY

Army Form C. 2118.

Place	Date	Hour	Summary of Events and Information	Remarks and references to Appendices
	20-21 night		went into the tunnels, 1 Coy in trenches on top; about 11 p.m. C Coy went forward to reinforce 68th Bde. & dug in on new B BLUE LINE or JASPER TRENCH. 4.30 p.m. Bath ordered to relieve 10th N.F.'s in BLUE LINE. 5.45 p.m. to 7 p.m. frantic shelling. relief complete 10 p.m.	
	21st		Coys dug in the whole night & by morning all coys had a continuous line of trench. B Coy formed defensive flank then our left of 13th D.L.I. to left of 11th D.W. Very heavy shelling throughout the day. 6.30 p.m. Enemy counter-attack. C Coy moved forward to strengthen B Coy, enemy did not reach our lines	
	22nd		Very heavy enemy shelling especially on Batt. H.Q. continual enemy artillery from 5 p.m. till 8 p.m. hurricane bombardment of our Buffs H.Q. & defensive flank TOWER HAMLETS.	
	23rd		Protective barrage 5.10 a.m. heavy bursts of enemy artillery throughout the day	
	24th		Protective barrage in early morning. heavy enemy shelling 5.15 a.m. & 7.30 p.m. c.p. to 7.30 p.m.	
	25-26 night		relieved by 11th SUSSEX in coy. complete 8.45 p.m. Enemy got to Bn. Bom. ?. & shelled heavily. Casualties during tour: Officers killed 1, wnd 7: O.Rs killed 22 Officers, killed 1, wnd 7 : O.Rs killed 22	

WAR DIARY or INTELLIGENCE SUMMARY

Army Form C. 2118.

Place	Date	Hour	Summary of Events and Information	Remarks and references to Appendices
	25th		wounded 83, missing 4.	
	26th		Batt at CHIPPAWA CAMP cleaning re-organising, etc.	
	27th		Inspection by Divisional General	
	28th		Proceeded to RIDGE WOOD on 5 p.m.	
	29th	10 a.m.	to BEDFORD HOUSE. 8.30 p.m. ordered to relieve 8th R.DUB.FUS in front line. Relief complete about 10 p.m. took over right sect., right Brigade. Relief slightly delayed by shelling. DISPOSITIONS: Front line C. Coy. Close support A. Coy. less 2 Platoons: counter-attack coy "D" Coy.: Batt reserve 2 Platoons A Coy + 2 Plats B. Coy. Gen. Reserve B. Coy less 2 Platoons.	
	30th		About 4 a.m. fog thick rose at 4.30 an intense bombardment helped a with machineguns & snake bombs. 5.15 a.m. enemy discovered in large numbers advancing against our front especially on our right. It must still have been thick, enemy seldom bombs & flammenwerfer. Heavy fire with rifles, Lewis & Machine Guns and bombs was opened on them & none reached our trench. S.O.S. sent up but [ ] was not seen at Batt. H.Q. owing to mist an adonk answered with the trench near at 7.20 a.m. About 6 a.m. enemy again attacked but was driven off: took 2 prisoners. 1 flammenwerfer & a machine-gun. 60 to 70 dead	

Army Form C. 2118.

WAR DIARY
or
INTELLIGENCE SUMMARY.
(Erase heading not required.)

Place	Date	Hour	Summary of Events and Information	Remarks and references to Appendices
			were left in front of our trenches, the attack was repulsed entirely with the fire of the infantry; the artillery did not barrage our front; a wire fence put up during the previous night by a pioneer batt. helped greatly to impede the enemy. A short barrage was put down on our lines at 10 a.m. the remainder of the day was normal	

WAR DIARY
or
INTELLIGENCE SUMMARY

Place	Date	Hour	Summary of Events and Information	Remarks and references to Appendices
MENIN RD	OCTOBER 1st		During night Sept 30th - Oct 1st front line barrage was increased by 3 series & was then returned. Sent to bar heavy enemy shelling on protective barrage opened 5.15am. S.O.S. went up on our left at 6am but no infantry action followed a our front. Heavily shelled about 12.30 pm especially round Batt. H.Q. Enemy aeroplanes active all day, flying low & firing at us. Fire was opened from the ground but without result.	
	2nd		6.30 pm enemy bombarded & at 7 pm was seen massing the artillery laid down the barrage heavily in reply to our S.O.S. & quashed the attack after this, the night was quiet. Protective barrage at dawn intermittent shelling during day. Relieved by 1 R. West Kents relief complete 11.45 pm	
			Casualties during tour. Killed 1 Officer 3 O.R. Wounded 1 Officer, 22 O.R's. Missing 3 O.R's.	
	3rd		Battalion moved to the METEREN AREA by bus, embussing at 2 pm and arriving in billets at 6 pm	
METEREN	4th to 8th		Kit, clothing Box Respirator, Rifle Inspections etc. - Specialists carried out training under their own officers. The commanding officer inspected the Bn on the 5th inst.	

WAR DIARY or INTELLIGENCE SUMMARY

Army Form C. 2118.

Place	Date	Hour	Summary of Events and Information	Remarks and references to Appendices
METEREN	6th		2nd Lt. D.H. WEBBE was transferred to England struck off the strength. Capt. C. Palmer relieves a Medical Board awaits.	
	7th		Struck off Strength – A.G's No. P/4984	
			The Bn attended a Brigade Church Parade. Numbers times were adopted on this date.	
	8th		All officers attended a lecture by the A.D.M.S. in the Y.M.C.A. hut at METEREN.	
	9th		Two companies fired on No. 2 Range with the other 2 companies carried on Musketry & Physical training and Bayonet fighting. A class for Junior N.C.O's under the R.S.M. was held during the morning. At 4 p.m. the Bn entrained for RIDGE WOOD arriving there at 11 p.m. and bivouacked for the night.	
	10th		At 2 pm the Bn marched into the front line and relieved the 11th Bn W. YORKS.	
	11.6.14		Casualties Capt S. Riddell killed. 2/Lt A.J. Walter & R. Cowley wounded 1 O.R. killed 7 O.R. wounded 4 O.R. ?missing believed killed Right of 14- to MICMAC CAMP.	

WAR DIARY or INTELLIGENCE SUMMARY

Army Form C. 2118.

Place	Date	Hour	Summary of Events and Information	Remarks and references to Appendices
	15&16		Major Grylls A.R. wounded to England 1-10-17. 2/Lt A Barker ditto 2-10-17. 2/Lt H.G. Smith ditto 29-9-17. 2/Lt J.E. Hall ditto 28-9-17.	
			MICMAC CAMP. Cleaning up. C.O.'s inspection. 2/Lt A. Hunt & W Darrall joined 15-: 2/Lt J Craven took sick. 2/Lt A.J. Wolton died of wounds 16-: Capt S.W. Moa took sick 15-.	
	17		Relieved 11 W Yorks & reserve Zillebeke Bund about 5.30 p.m.	
	18		Batt moved to line & relieved 8 KOYLI. 2/Lt S. Wheeliker to England	
	20		Bt relieved by 11 W Yorks. Batt H.Q. (Rd) Coys to BUND. A Coy relieved coy of 11 W.Y. in Jhr a. & became Batt. on 6.8 yd. C.Coy to about I.S.E. & Aft 6 11 W.Y. Total casualties to town 4 O.R. killed 20 O.R. wounded.	
	21		To Bravena Camp 22" Cleaning up. 2/Lt H Park to Engr. conf. 22-10-17	
	23		Batt less A & C Coys embossed at Dickebush Sta. for Nazenus — en detraining to billets. E squadron area arrived 5.30 pm. A.Q's lecture. B.D. Coys E Cluidenthom Cleaning up. A & C Coys arrived. C.O.'s inspection. 2/Lt N.S. Wilson & R.C.M Douthwaite joined 18-10-17. 2/Lt A Hyggs rejoined 25-10-17. 2/Lt F Kempster & R Roberts joined 24-10-17. 2/Lt A. & Q.M. Bell to England 26-10-17 & struck off strength.	
	24		In this area magazines of brook were carried out close order drill, P.T. Arms Drill	

A6045 Wt. W11422/M1160. 350000. 12/16 D.D.&L. Forms/C/2118/14.

WAR DIARY
or
INTELLIGENCE SUMMARY.
(Erase heading not required.)

Army Form C. 2118.

Place	Date	Hour	Summary of Events and Information	Remarks and references to Appendices
	28		Specialists trained. G.O.C. Brigade inspected billets 2.6—; stables inspected by M.O. Range practice 27ᵗʰ at Quebec. 7ᵗʰ Battn. in Wigginson 2.15 p- arrived 5 p.m. Instructors arrived to recall all men on leave, Canada etc.	
	29		G.O.C. Div. inspected bath 10 a.m. Draft of 9 O.Rs. joined	
	30		Range practice for the Draft. Leaving up ete for Ex Chaplain 2ⁿᵈ W.T.C. inspected	
	31		C-in-C inspected the Brigade. Drafts of 50 O.R. + 75 O.R. joined	

Hunstreet ?/Lt. Comdt
4.4.17